DEATH RIDE
FROM FENCHURCH STREET
and other
VICTORIAN RAILWAY
MURDERS

DEATH RIDE
FROM FENCHURCH STREET
and other
VICTORIAN RAILWAY
MURDERS

ARTHUR & MARY SELLWOOD

AMBERLEY

First published 1979 by David & Charles Ltd.
This edition 2009.

Amberley Publishing Plc
Cirencester Road, Chalford,
Stroud, Gloucestershire, GL6 8PE

www.amberley-books.com

British Library Cataloguing in Publication Data.
A catalogue record for this book is available from the British Library.

ISBN 978 1 84868 495 9

Typesetting and Origination by Diagraf (www.diagraf.net)
Printed in Great Britain

Contents

List of Illustrations

Foreword

Like many of the trains of the era it portrays, this account of murder on the Victorian railways took a long time to get started and is somewhat late in its arrival.

It was just after World War II that a certain Miss Pill, then a sprightly lady in her late nineties, first aroused our interest in the subject by revealing to Mary, sent by a local newspaper to interview her, that she was related to a Mr Gold, murdered' on the Brighton line in 1881.

Miss Pill's account of the crime was so vivid and so absorbing in its evocative portrayal of an age that, until then, we had regarded as remote and rather dull. But it was only quite recently, following a violent incident on a night train, that the idea she had given us really got up steam.

A regular commuter, I suddenly realised that, since the end of the fifties, my annual travel tally totalled some thirty thousand miles, the equivalent – over the past twenty years – of twenty-five times around the Earth, or a return trip, plus a single, to the Moon. And, so far, I had achieved this staggering mileage without fear or thought that there might be any particular hazard on the way.

But how did the timid passenger feel – or fare – in the days when, instead of 'open-plan' compartments and corridor coaches, he was isolated in his individual wooden box, with such comforting reassurances as communication cords and electric lighting only the palest of gleams in an inventor's eye?

And just how did the police forces of the time, when forensic medicine was in its infancy and finger-printing unknown, ever manage to corner, as they did, the killers who took advantage of this awful vulnerability of the traveller?

If, in *Death Ride from Fenchurch Street*, we have managed to convey to the reader, however imperfectly, some picture of what to us has become a most intriguing period in the history of our railways – and our country – then our thanks are due to those who helped us in our efforts to that end.

We would particularly mention our good friends in the East Sussex County Records Office, the British Transport Police, the East Sussex County Library, the library of the London Borough of Sutton, Wallington Reference Library, the National Railway Museum at York, the Public Relations Department of British Rail, Eastern Region, the Public Lending Library, Seaford, Sussex, and the newspaper library at the Daily Mirror.

Without their enthusiastic advice and ungrudging aid our narrative might well have gone off the rails, and it would most certainly have run out of fuel!

Arthur Sellwood
Seaford, Sussex
1979

The North London Railway: it was in a carriage like this that the first murder on Britain's railways took place.

1

Death Ride from Fenchurch Street

It was so soon after 9.30 on the night of Saturday 9 July 1864 that the bells of the ancient City churches were still swaying from their exertions in having struck the half hour, when an elderly gentleman of prosperous appearance alighted from the horse omnibus that had brought him to King William Street from the Old Kent Road and crossed over into Eastcheap; thence he proceeded importantly, but with no unseemly show of haste, towards Mark Lane and the graceful metal verandah that, topped by a row of tall arched windows, marked the entrance to Fenchurch Street Station.

Knowing that the train that was to take him home to the prosperous suburb of Hackney was not due to leave until 9.50, the traveller had plenty of time to spare as, walking stick firmly in one hand, and neat travelling bag in the other, he strode through the booking hall towards the double staircase that led up to the platforms. He was a man who never hurried: hurry was never necessary. A flibbertigibbet might leave things to chance; the prudent lived according to their Bradshaws.

It was a dark night, unnaturally so considering the time of the year, and made even darker by the clouds of smoke and steam that belched from the tall chimney of the engine. The steam exploded noisily against the pillars of brick and iron that, soot-stained over the twenty years since the station had been built, flanked the platform used for the traffic of the North London Railway.

Even the gas lamps, which had just been lit, did little to alleviate the unseasonable man-made gloom, their wan light served simply to enlarge the size of the shadows cast by those who passed beneath them.

The newspaper vendor, shouting his wares outside the station entrance was later to recall 'it fair gave you the creeps' but, if the traveller shared his feelings he did not show it.

At sixty-nine, Thomas Briggs, chief clerk of Robarts Bank in Lombard Street, was not one to indulge in fanciful forebodings. Benign of expression and calmly precise – if also perhaps a shade pompous – he was no stranger to the station or its moods. When he took his place in the first-class compartment towards the centre of the train it was as one performing a well-practised rite.

Every Saturday night since the death of his wife, just seven years before, Mr Briggs would make a punctual pilgrimage to Peckham – a once-weekly visit to a married niece – and never once did he fail to return in good time for the train that would carry him home to Clapton Square, Hackney, where he lived with his son.

A gentleman of methodical habits, the station staff rightly theorised. A gentleman who regulated his movements, and his comfort, by careful reference to the clock, or rather the bland dial of the well-polished gold watch that, its heavy chain supporting a swivel seal and two small keys, formed a cupid's bow between his two vest pockets. That watch was correct, or so he would gently boast, to 'every blessed fraction of a minute'.

As the whistle blew, the driver opened his regulator, and the little tank locomotive, its bright burnished dome reflecting the glare from the open firedoor, began to puff and pant towards the open. Guard Ames little thought that this was the last time the 9.50 would carry Mr Briggs, let alone that he himself would be a prosecution witness when a man stood accused of the widower's murder.

Scheduled time for the 9.50's journey between Fenchurch Street and Hackney was twenty minutes. There were only two stops, at Bow and Hackney Wick, the latter more commonly known as Victoria Park. Having spent the evening in 'taking a stroll' and, as he later confessed under cross-examination, a 'glass of ale' (or so) in the local pub, Tom Lee, described as a 'gentleman of independent means' boarded the train at the first stop, and doubtless later wished that he had not.

According to his subsequent statement to the court, Lee, as he moved along the platform to the second-class coach immediately behind the engine, had caught sight of Mr Briggs, a neighbour of his, sitting in his customary seat in the leading 'first'. Thanks to the carriage having stopped alongside one of the station's gas lamps, Lee had also been able to observe that the traveller was not alone. There were two other men in the coach, or so he claimed, one at Briggs' side and the other sitting opposite. However, there had been 'no sign of anything wrong' and having exchanged a cheery good night with the banker as he passed, he had devoted no further thought to the episode until he had read about the murder in the newspapers.

However, by the time that this 'gentleman' witness – of whom more later – condescended, under police pressure, to tell his story, practically every man and woman in the country had heard of the unfortunate Thomas Briggs, and Scotland Yard had begun a murder hunt that, for its size and scope, was then unprecedented in English legal history.

'The murder of Thomas Briggs', states *The Annual Register* for 1864, 'will be long remembered as one of the most notable events of the year – a crime which seemed to bring home to every citizen in the United Kingdom, no matter how quiet and orderly his life, the danger of a sudden and violent death.'

Such depressing reflections, however, were far removed from the minds of Messrs Verney and Sidney James as they boarded the train at Hackney. Young gentlemen clerks, and belonging by odd coincidence to the same establishment as Mr Briggs, they enjoyed the role of roistering blades during their leisure hours, regrettably scant though those leisure hours might be. Intent on a good night out they had booked first class for Highbury, on the next stage of the 9.50's run.
But scarcely had they seated themselves than one of them remarked that the thick leather seat cushion was wet and sticky to the touch and, on examining his hand, was horrified to find that it was smeared with blood. A moment later his companion exclaimed 'There's blood on the seat as well ...' The travellers rushed out of the carriage and yelled to the guard only seconds before the train was due to start.

Guard Ames was more than a little flustered as he hurried along the platform to answer their call. The 9.50 had been five minutes late arriving at Fenchurch Street on its earlier run and, try though the driver did to make up this lost time, it had still been four minutes late on arrival at Hackney. On the North London Railway such tardiness was a rare offence indeed. Ames didn't want to lose more time through the North London suburbs.

Although the NLR'S territory extended only over the eight miles that lay between Chalk Farm and Blackwall (plus the Broad Street line opened in 1865), it boasted no fewer than eighteen stations along its route and the little railway was intensely proud of the service it offered.

The new terminus of the Blackwall Railway at Fenchurch Street, December 1853
(Courtesy the Mansell Collection)

Its trains also ran over other railways including the short-lived service to Fenchurch Street.

The NLR'S team of spruce tank locomotives, liveried in bright green 'with black bands and red lines' around their burnished bodies, and its smartly turned-out carriages, each one of them bearing on its doorpanel the company's colourful and somewhat flamboyant crest, set a standard of comfort and design that few of its big contemporaries could equal.

For, conscious though it was of its sterling virtues it was also eminently respectful to its patrons: the affluent Briggses and their kind who, in increasing numbers, were moving house away from the city smoke to settle in the pleasant countryside east of Bow.

Not for the Briggses were the wheeled coffins that so often made travel a misery for the third-class passenger on other far larger railways. The NLR refused, until the mid 1870s, to carry third-class passengers. 'Our clients', as one of the company's directors somewhat loftily intoned, 'are all of a class that can afford to travel first or second ...' As such they demanded – and were given – creature comfort. Punctuality was taken for granted.

Ames' personal forebodings on this latter score, and his frustration at the summons from the clerks as likely to cause further delay, disappeared as soon as his handlamp threw a little more light on the scene inside the carriage. The first thing that caught his eye was the hat that lay on the floor between the seats. It was a hat of an unusual type and shape, cut low above the crown. Next was the blood, in patches on the cushions. And then peering below the seats he found a small travelling bag and a walking stick, blood thinly filming its silver knob.

There was blood on the door. Blood on the doorhandle. Blood near the hat.

Turning to the would-be revellers, both of them now grave-faced and more than a little frightened, Ames said respectfully: 'I think, gentlemen, we're going to have a bit of a wait, and I must trouble you to give me your names and addresses ...'

He pulled up the carriage windows, locked the door and then telegraphed his news to Camden Town. Violent robbery, perhaps even murder, had been perpetrated. Of that he was sure. But where – and who – was the victim?

Twenty minutes later Driver Elkin supplied the answer.

Taking a string of empty coaches back to Fenchurch Street between Hackney Wick and Bow, Driver Elkin was appalled to see a 'dark mound' piled across the track ahead of him. Immediately he applied the brake and slowly the train came to a shuddering halt. It had been a close shave, the closest he had known. The locomotive's buffers were only a few feet from the mound; a few feet more and it would have ploughed right into it.

When Elkin climbed down from the footplate and, together with Guard Timms, went to examine this unexpected obstacle he found that it was a man, alive, but terribly battered and unconscious. He was bleeding profusely, and they had great difficulty in even lifting him off the track. Their cries for help were answered by people living in the houses that backed on to the railway, and, narrowly escaping being run down by an approaching train, they managed to carry him to the Milford Castle, a nearby pub. There Guard Timms accepted a pint of beer, and so did Elkin even though still on duty. Frown though his bosses might at such a breach of discipline, he felt he had earned his drink.

Meanwhile, Police Constable Edward Duggan, attracted by the shouts of Elkin's party, had arrived on the scene and now started to search the man's clothes to find a clue to his identity. He was obviously a man of considerable substance: a gentleman. There were four sovereigns and some keys in his left-hand pocket, 10s 6d in silver in the other. He also had on his person a silver snuff-box, and on his well-manicured finger was a diamond ring.

But only when the PC read the letters that he carried in his jacket, was the injured man identified as Thomas Briggs, and only after his son had been brought from Clapton Square was the link established between the bag and the blood-stained stick recovered by Guard Ames. The bag was the banker's own and the stick was one that young Mr Briggs had lent him; but the hat belonged to neither – the hat was a mystery.

A black beaver with a low flat crown, the hat found in the carriage was certainly not the type of headgear that would have been worn by staid Briggs senior. Mr Briggs, as his son explained, had always been 'fussy' in his choice of hat, and in that respect had even been a trifle vain. Each year he had a hat especially made for him by Messrs Dignance, an exclusive City hatters, next to the Royal Exchange.

He had been wearing the latest of these acquisitions – a shining topper – when he had embarked the previous morning for his fateful visit to Peckham: yet now there was no trace of it. Neither was there any sign of his cherished gold watch, nor of its matching chain, except a gold fastening from which it had been torn.

Conducted in the light of the gas mantles in the parlour of the pub, and accompanied by the rumbling and whistling of the passing trains, this inspection of the banker's wounds and his personal possessions was a macabre investigation. Mr Briggs himself was still unconscious, and was to remain so, unable to utter a single word regarding his attacker. Later he was taken home, where he was attended by his own physician; but all efforts to revive him were in vain and he was dead before nightfall.

On the face of it the task confronting the police was a thoroughly hopeless one. The only clue to Mr Briggs' assailant was that odd-shaped hat, evidently abandoned in the confusion of the struggle that had led to the banker's death. But with the male population of the time totalling something like ten million, and probably a quarter of them members of the hat brigade, the chances of finding its owner were slim indeed.

Yet scant though the clue might be, Inspector Tanner – sent from the Yard to take over the case from K Division – was determined to make the most of it. By the following morning an artist's drawing of the hat, together with a description of the murdered Mr Briggs and an account of his last-known movements, was on prominent display outside every police station in the Metropolitan area.

Notices were also posted outside the main railway stations and then, to harness self-interest to the cause of public spiritedness, the police advertised a reward of £100. This offer was quickly duplicated by Robarts Bank, shocked at the fate of so respected an employee and, after a boardroom discussion, the North London Railway added a similar sum.

But Tanner was not content with printed appeals alone. Soon hat shops by the score were being visited by weary but patient PCs seeking a 'match' to the abandoned hat. London's myriad pawnbrokers were circularised with details of the dead man's watch and chain. And the Press, its imagination fired by the awful precedent afforded by 'Murder on the Iron Way', as the ballad-mongers put it, gave the affair an almost unprecedented publicity.

The newspapers – true blue or vulgar yellow as the case might be – were for once not guilty of the charge, levelled at them in Victorian times almost as frequently as today, of originating and shaping the prejudices and fears of those who read them. Instead they were merely echoing current public opinion.

Until then it had been fondly imagined that crime, major crime, on the railways was confined to foreign parts, in particular the United States and France. Bar the acute discomfiture endured in the crowded, unheated and unlit third-class compartments that catered for the 'industrious poor', the traveller on English railways had little to fear but derailment or collision: or so it had been assumed. Shattering as it did this insular complacency, the Briggs murder not only brought disillusion, but speedily created something closely resembling panic.

As Sergeant Parry, one of the most notable counsels of the age was later to proclaim to a crowded court: 'The crime … is almost unparalleled in this country. It is a crime which strikes at the lives of millions. It is a crime which affects the life of every man who travels upon the great iron ways of this country … a crime of a character to arouse in the human breast an almost instinctive spirit of vengeance.'

And as the Solicitor General was to pronounce to an awed and receptive jury: 'If there is any occasion when a man may consider himself perfectly safe it is when he is travelling in a first-class railway carriage in the metropolis … a most extraordinary crime.'

But by then a man would be on trial for his life; a man called Franz Muller, destined to make fashionable, through his notoriety, the Muller

Hat. And one of the first to testify against him would be a witness whose own name was to become almost equally celebrated, in this case for its sinister portent of the prisoner's fate. The witness's name was DEATH.

John Death – he preferred the word to be pronounced as Deeth – was the principal of a jewellers and silversmiths in Cheapside and not only sold to customers but also bought from them. Though this latter activity was not one which, as a city gentleman, he chose to brag about, or unduly advertise, Mr Death was well known to those in need of turning their property into cash.

It was at ten o' clock on the morning of the 11th, less than thirty-six hours after the unfortunate Briggs had breathed his last, that the jeweller was confronted by an earnest young man who presented for his inspection and valuation a gold watch-chain.

Though cool and collected in manner, the caller seemed anxious to stay in the shadows: not once did he place himself in a position where he was exposed to full view. Death also noted his accent, which he identified as German, and his disappointment when told that the chain, though attractive, was not worth more than £3 10s. This struck the shrewd jeweller as curious. To one of the young man's apparent class and circumstances £3 10s should have been a considerable sum. He decided he had best be 'careful' over the deal. £3 10s he had said. £3 10s it would remain.

But what most surprised Death was when his visitor asked for an exchange of goods instead of cash, and suggested he be given a chain priced at £3 17s 6d. Finally, however – this being refused – he reluctantly settled for another chain at £3 5s and then took a gold ring with a white stone in it, to make up the 5s difference.

Probably more than a little glad to see the back of this odd customer, for the transaction had taken over fifteen minutes to complete, Death placed the chain he had just sold in a jewel box with the name of the shop on its lid, wrapped this in tissue paper and, handing it to the young man, bade him goodday.

Neither jeweller nor customer could anticipate at that moment the remarkable events to which this routine 'parcelling' would give rise. As a certain Fleet Street scribe was to picturesquely put it, Muller had left the shop with his *death* notice in his pocket …

It was the very next day that the jeweller, receiving the description of Mr Briggs' missing watch and chain was struck by its resemblance to the one he had just purchased. Spurred by the thought of the murder, and no doubt the promised reward, he promptly reported the transaction to the police.

Yet even though the chain was then duly identified by Briggs junior as having belonged to his father, the Yard still had little to work on as regards the identity of the murderer. Death's description of the customer's appearance was necessarily vague, and probably would have fitted a million of the city's artisans. All that he could be positive about was that distinctive German accent, and for this the police team had to be grateful.

They circulated the description – such as it was – and publicized the story in the Press in the faint hope that some chance passer-by might have seen the suspect leave the shop. In the event, however, it was the jeweller's box, spotted by a cab-driver – one James Matthews – that led the law to put a name upon its quarry.

According to Matthews' story – later to be hotly contested by the defence – the first he heard of the North London Railway murder was on Thursday 20 July, a full eleven days after its occurrence. He said that a fellow driver had told him about it when he had taken his horse to a horse trough, and had drawn his attention to a 'Wanted' placard posted nearby.

Immediately the name of Death the jewellers had caught his eye as the name on a box he had seen his small daughter playing with a couple of days before. This had been given to her by an acquaintance of the family, a young German tailor called Franz Muller. And then, said Matthews, he had studied the description of the hat found in the railway carriage and had found that, if the box had been familiar, the hat was even more so. 'You will probably find the hat to be Muller's too,' he told detectives.

Matthews claimed that some months earlier Muller had admired the novel shape of a hat he had bought at Messrs Walker of Marylebone, and had asked him – as the shop was on his cab run – if he could get him a similar one, but of a size smaller. This Matthews had duly done, and had been given in exchange a fancy waistcoat and other items from the young tailor's wardrobe. This hat, the cabman said, was identical in appearance with the one found on the train.

Nor was this – important though it was – the sole service that Matthews was able to offer the police. He also obligingly provided them with a photograph of his erstwhile 'friend', and told them that he lodged with a Mr and Mrs Blyth in Old Ford Road, Victoria Park. However, when Tanner called there he found no sign of his man. He

Two portraits of Franz Muller, murderer of Thomas Briggs, who was executed in 1864.

had left his lodgings, and had quit the country as well. He was now at sea, on his way to America.

A strong pointer to the latter's guilt? It certainly failed to impress the Blyths as such. They had nothing but good to say about their former lodger. He was 'affectionate and kind'. He was 'mild-mannered and always polite'. They were staggered to hear that he was being 'looked for' by the police. They were convinced he must be the victim of a tragic mistake. For Muller's journey, they insisted, was no frenzied last-minute bid to escape the law. He had been telling them a good fortnight before the murder of his intention to emigrate.

Nor had there been any sign of guilt or extra nervousness about him when they had talked with him on the day after the murder. On the contrary, he had been in extraordinarily good spirits. He had told them that at last he had the fare money with which to embark on his cherished project, and had even gone so far as to name the ship on which he'd sail, the sailing ship *Victoria*, bound for New York.

'In fact', said Mrs Blyth, 'he has since written to us' and she produced for the astonished detective a letter to prove it.

'On the sea, July 16th', was the dateline of Muller's dispatch, written in disarmingly fractured English and posted in Worthing as the *Victoria* took her last look at home. It was bright and cheerful in tone, assuring his 'dear friends' that 'I cannot have a better time as I have, for the sun shines nice and the wind blows fair as it is at present moment'. Everything, he said 'will go well'.

Coming from a man supposedly fleeing the country after perpetrating a particularly brutal murder, such frankness concerning his whereabouts and destination was indeed unusual. Yet the apparent candour of the epistle, which concluded (very much in keeping with its author's usual form) with a request to the Blyths to pay the postage, cut little ice with the enquiring Tanner.

The photograph supplied by Matthews had been shown to Mr Death, who had identified it as resembling the man who had sold him Briggs' watch-chain. And now, when the Blyths were asked if their lodger had left any of his possessions behind him, Mrs Blyth produced a hat-box. It bore on it the name of Walker, the shop where Matthews claimed to have bought Muller that 'unusual' hat.

'That clinches it. He's our man', the Inspector exclaimed. All the same, there were formidable obstacles against his quarry's apprehension. Thanks to the cabman's delay in producing his evidence, Muller had a head start, and a very substantial one. Already he had been several days at sea.

In addition, once he touched American soil, the process of extraditing him might prove to be somewhat complicated. America was locked in civil war, and relationships between the Northern States and Britain, accused of favouring the Confederates, had seldom been more strained. Following the ravages of the raider *Alabama* – built in Britain and partly manned by a British crew – anglophobia was raging among the Federal leaders, certain of whom were pressing the President to go so far as to declare a state of war.

In view of such special factors it was decided at the Home Office that there was no recourse but for Tanner to go to New York in person, and take the chief witnesses – Matthews and Death along with him. And he, for his part, decided that he must get there before the *Victoria* docked and Muller could lose himself among the millions. There was, it was true, no chance of effecting this objective if he travelled by sailing ship: but say he tried to see what could be done by steam?

Less than twelve hours after the Blyths had shown him the hatbox, Tanner, accompanied by Detective Sergeant Clarke and his two ill-assorted witnesses, left for Liverpool to embark on the steamship *City of Manchester*. In the pocket of the Inspector's frockcoat was a warrant from the chief magistrate at Bow Street for Muller's arrest on the charge of murder.

It was not until the morning of 25 August that the *Victoria* entered the mouth of the Hudson River and hove to off New York harbour, to await the arrival of a pilot. For a certain young German among the steerage passengers it was a moment to be savoured, the turning-point, or so he imagined, in a career that, until then, had failed singularly to satisfy his earlier expectations.

To those who had encountered him back in London, Franz Muller had seemed, though short in stature, a 'cut above' the classes among whom he lived and worked when it came to his aspirations. A native of Saxe-Weimar, he had started his career as apprentice to a gunsmith and had come to England only after failing to find an outlet for his specialised skills at home. But two years in the metropolis had left him as far as ever from his goal of setting up as a gunsmith on his own. In fact, the only post available to him had been that of a jobbing tailor which, while sufficient to provide him with a living, was quite inadequate to meet the bills that arose from his near-obsessive vanity.

Always a 'sharp dresser', he was habitually embarrassed by the fact that, to keep up with fashion, he must live beyond his means, and even more embarrassed by the consequences of his frequent resort to the pawnbroker as a means of temporarily enlarging them.

When still a young man whose first 'trifling pieces', as he called them, were yet to appear in print, Charles Dickens had observed that 'of the numerous receptacles for misery and distress with which the streets of London unhappily abound, there are perhaps none which present such striking scenes as the pawnbrokers shops'.

Had he been acquainted with Sketches by Boz, Franz Muller would have recognised that – three decades later – the description still held good. Equally would he have agreed with the great novelist's reflection that: 'There are grades of pawning, as in everything else ... so the better sort of pawnbroker calls himself a silversmith and decorates his shop with handsome trinkets and expensive ·jewellery. While the more humble moneylender boldly advertises his calling and invites observation.'

The discreetly genteel ... the ruthlessly blatant ... Muller had experienced each of them, but now, as he gazed eagerly at the shores of the land he had for so long envisaged as his personal El Dorado, it is unlikely that his thoughts strayed even momentarily to the seedy setting of his last 'financing', the wooden-walled cubicle presided over by Mrs Barker of Houndsditch.

Certainly it would not have occurred to him that a visit he had paid to that shabby little shop, its nature advertised only by the three golden balls above the barred fanlight of its door, had been reported, over a month before, to a tenacious hound of the law by the name of Tanner. Nor that that persevering and determined character had then examined the article pawned – a gold watchchain – and found that it coincided with that 'exchanged' by Messrs Death for the watch-chain of the late Mr Briggs. Muller's mind was set on the future.

He had raised £1 15s as a result of his negotiations with Mother Barker, and had then sold the pawn-ticket for just 10s more. Together these transactions had improved his fortunes sufficiently for him to be able to pay his passage money – £4 5s for a one-way trip – and as such he must have considered them to be highly satisfactory. How was he to know that these same transactions were now helping to tighten the noose around his unsuspecting neck?

Despite his cheerful letter to the Blyths the young German had found the voyage far from trouble-free. That £4 5s had been supposed to cover not only his fare, but also his food and drink while aboard ship, but predictably it had done nothing of the sort. He had actually run short of money and, as he later claimed, had been forced to sell some of his clothes in order barely to survive.

On one occasion he had tried to raise cash by taking a bet that he could eat five pounds of German sausage at a single sitting. To pay for his subsequent failure he had to call for drinks all round.

Financially embarrassed as he was, there had been times when the Blyths' 'mild-mannered' ex-lodger had found himself so sorely tried that he had resorted to outbreaks of temper and vulgar abuse. Indeed, he had even become involved in a fight with a fellow passenger and had received a black eye for calling him a liar and a robber.

Yet from the moment the *Victoria's* passengers had first caught sight of the American seaboard, Muller had relegated his sorrows to the past. To his fellow passengers in the steerage class he seemed cheerful, energetic, ebullient and charming: full of talk about the opportunities ahead. It was a mood, however, that was not destined to last.

With the rest of his companions still gathered on deck, Muller decided to return to his cabin and collect his gear together, preparatory to his going ashore. As a result he did not hear the shouts and jeers from the crowd aboard a passing excursion steamer that so puzzled his fellow passengers: shouts and jeers of 'Muller the murderer'. Nor did he see the figures who thronged the deck of the oncoming pilot boat, among them his old acquaintances, the cabman Matthews with, at his side, the jeweller called Death.

Muller's illusions about what the New World had to offer came to an abrupt and brutal ending when, within minutes of the pilot boat's arrival alongside, he was requested to accompany one of the ship's officers aft, and found himself confronted by three men who were strangers to him.

For a moment or two they stared at him as if studying his reactions, but said nothing; then one of them, stepping forward, asked abruptly, 'Your name is Franz Muller?'

His face paled as he answered, 'I am he.'

The man grabbed him by the arm with one hand, and, brandished a piece of parchment in the other.

'Why, what's the matter?' stammered the German. 'What is happening?'

Another of the men stepped forward and, in an American accent said, 'You are charged with the murder of Mr Thomas Briggs.'

Then, evidently uncertain about how to proceed, he paused and Detective Sergeant Clarke obligingly followed up with the information 'on the North London Railway between Hackney Wick and Bow on the 9th of July'.

'But,' protested Muller, 'I was never on that line.'

Clarke merely shrugged. 'This gentleman', indicating the man with the accent, 'is Mr John Ternan, a police detective from New York.'

The three then took their prisoner, still protesting, down into the saloon, extracted from his pocket the key to his 'cabin trunk' – a large black box – and, rummaging among his belongings, made two interesting finds. One was a once-elegant topper, with the initials 'DD' pencilled on its band. The other was a heavy gold watch.

'How long have you had these items?' Clarke demanded.

'I have had the watch about two years, and the hat about twelve months', Muller answered.

It was a lie that was to cost him dear.

The *City of Manchester* had made swift progress. While the *Victoria*, her sails limp as shrouds, had lain becalmed for days on end, the steamer, billowing huge clouds of smoke and cinders, had overtaken and passed her quarry and arrived in New York a good fortnight ahead of her.

But Tanner and Clarke had been far from idle during this period of waiting. Anxious to guard against the chance of the sailing ship's arrival ahead of schedule, and fearful lest their suspect might slip ashore, they haunted the wharfside and the pilot's office, and daily visited their opposite numbers in the New York City Police.

Back in England their work had been necessarily undercover. Here there was no need for secrecy, or so they felt. In an age where no direct communication existed between ship and shore, no link to alert their suspect as to what awaited him at the end of his voyage, it paid, so Tanner reasoned, to be frank in his dealings with the authorities and the Press, and generous in hospitality to informants.

On this sunny August morning the British team had every reason for self-congratulation: their strategy of publicising both crime and suspect had worked exactly as planned. True, as Tanner confessed, there had been moments of doubt: the most notable being when the crowd on that accursed excursion steamer had nearly blown the gaff. Indeed, as the pilot boat approached the *Victoria* the hearts of the plain-clothes officers had sunk into their heavy black boots for fear that their man-alerted by the din would elude justice by suicide, or, even worse, would swim ashore. Now that such fears had proved groundless they could savour their triumph.

On the other hand, any thought they may have entertained that all they had left to do was to apply for an extradition certificate in order for it to be promptly granted, and thus enable them to accompany the suspect on the next boat home, was to be speedily shattered by the shore's reaction to their coup.

Innocently, they had hitherto assumed that any opposition to the Crown's request for Muller's return to Britain for his trial would be based purely on considerations of law – and the argument be confined to the nature of the crime and the evidence pointing to Muller as its perpetrator. The political climate ruled otherwise.

Only three months earlier, the celebrated *Alabama* had at last met her end off Cherbourg, sunk by the USS *Kearsarge*, but not before she had been on the rampage in four oceans, and claimed scores of Northern merchantmen as her victims. And then, to add further insult to injury, a large number of her crew had been snatched from captivity by the audacious intervention of an English yacht.

Thanks to the feelings aroused by this episode, plus the agitation of the immigrant Irish, with which New York abounded, and the pressures of the opulent German-American societies, always ready to rally around a kinsman, Tanner had a tougher task ahead than even the Home and Foreign Office experts anticipated.

What with congressmen courting popularity through twisting the lion's tail, and local journalists jumping on the bandwagon in the most purple of purple prose, the plight of Franz Muller, now that all America had heard of it, was to invoke considerations far removed from the fate of poor, prosaic Thomas Briggs, awaiting respectable interment in an East London grave.

The extradition proceedings opened on the 26th, presided over by Commissioner Newton. Fireworks were expected.

Against the British Consul, Frederick Marbury, was pitted the redoubtable Chauncey Schaffer, whose verbal pyrotechnics had long been gratefully celebrated in the patriot Press. You could always rely on 'Schaff' the newsmen said, to provide good-selling 'copy'. In his handling of the Muller case he promised to exceed even the best of his admirers' expectations. And when he rose to address the court on the second day of the hearing, he solemnly asserted that its proceedings were invalid. England and the United States were in a state of war!

'An undeclared war', he added, 'but nonetheless a state of war. A mixed and unsolemn state of war, as Groetus defined it. A state of things that, by the common consent of mankind, suspends all treaties between the two countries concerned.'

But this was only a taste of the feast to come.

Never before had the district courtroom been favoured by such a variegated crowd. People of all classes, and of no class at all, packed the public benches; hundreds of others gathered outside. Intrigued by both the novel nature of the crime, and the political fuss surrounding the fate of the suspected criminal, it was an audience that expected much, and was not to be disappointed.

'England', cried the eloquent advocate, 'cannot say she is neutral when she furnishes our rebellious subjects with vessels of war, opens her ports to them, furnishes them with arms and ammunition and sends them forth on their errand of destruction ...'

At this stage his words were almost drowned by public applause. The detectives, who had expected the argument to be concerned with such matters as the geography of the railway line between Fenchurch Street and Hackney, or how brightly a gas lamp on a station platform could illuminate the inside of a first-class carriage of a train that had stopped at Bow, found themselves treated instead to a dissertation upon the depredations of the *Alabama* and her fellow raider, the *Florida*.

'Robbers on the High Seas', thundered Chauncey Schaffer, pointing an accusing finger at the startled Tanner, as if the police inspector had hoisted the skull and cross-bones. 'Murdering our citizens, destroying our commerce and humiliating our nation ...'

Once again his audience (unrebuked by the bench) showed its appreciation in the traditional way.

In later years, Schaffer's critics were to assert that his style was far too emotional. Tanner would doubtless have employed a less polite description. But certainly the attorney gave the crowd its money's worth.

His address extended over several thousand words and took in practically every aspect of Anglo-American discord. From the 'conspiracy' of English aristocrats against the young republic, to the raids by exiled confederates slipping across the Canadian border, each point of conflict was cited in support of his persistent argument: that the extradition treaty was 'a dead letter' until the British had repented of-and ceased-their wickedness.

'England', Schaffer said, 'must come into Court with clean hands. She must not come here and ask of us to honour her justice when she dishonours her own, breaks her treaties and cries peace and neutrality while, at the same time, she lets slip the dogs of war ... this cannot long continue.'

And he even went so far in his peroration as to say: 'Better for us we had war at once, when we could send out our cruisers and assert our rights of retaliation on the ocean. The pride and courage of America is at stake.'

It was powerful stuff, and rapturously received. Schaffer sat down amid a storm of cheers. It also made good newspaper copy. Despite news of the giant battles then raging on every front, the *New York Herald* found space for nearly every word of it, and it travelled, via the news agencies, throughout the warring states. It aroused fury in Canada, smug approval in Germany, and became overnight the major topic of every New York bar.

But, unfortunately for the man on whose behalf so much martial eloquence had been mustered – the pale-faced man in the dock – it failed in the ultimate to impress Commissioner Newton.

When it was the prosecution's turn to address the court, Marbury, who had listened to Schaffer's dramatic assault upon his government with a carefully studied appearance of incredulity and boredom, excused himself from 'the necessity of even as much as adverting to many of the irrelevant matters which the gentleman who has just spoken has dragged into the discussion'.

It was not for the court to decide whether the treaty under which the accused was claimed was faithfully observed or not. All that was immaterial.

'So long as the governments of the two countries regard the treaty as a subsisting treaty,' he continued, 'it holds its place under the Constitution, and· it would be trifling with the time of the court to pursue this point any further.'

And in final contemptuous dismissal of his opponent's arguments he added: 'The only excuse or apology counsel could possibly offer for the introduction of such topics must be the fact that the case offers, on its own merits, no entertainment to the audience.'

So into the argument came such matters as the timetable of the North London Railway, the distance between its stations, and the description of the two mysterious passengers allegedly seen in Briggs' carriage on the train's arrival at Bow.

The evidence of Death the jeweller was presented concerning the exchange of the murdered man's watch-chain, and the reappearance in Mrs Barker's pawnshop of the chain for which it had been exchanged. Matthew's testimony was also cited, and Marbury dwelt heavily on the significance of the hats.

Much was made of the fact that the hat found on the train had been made by Messrs Walker 'and proved by witnesses to have belonged to Muller, and to have been worn by him up to the time of the murder or nearly so'.

Before leaving for America, Tanner had managed to obtain a deposition from a Mrs Repsch to the effect that, on the night following the murder, Muller had appeared in a 'nearly new hat' with a white silk lining. In answer to her jocular comment on his extravagance he had replied, or so she said, that his old one had been thrown into a dust-hole.

Much was also made of the fact that Briggs' own hat had been taken by the murderer, and could well be the one found among his belongings aboard ship. And also produced in court was that heavy gold watch: a watch made by Archer of Hackney, only a few streets away from Mr Briggs' home.

'This is the chain of evidence complete,' concluded Marbury. 'With not a link wanting to connect the prisoner with the commission of the crime.'

By the time the Consul sat down it was evident that his cool summary of the facts had deeply impressed the court, and had temporarily subdued even the noisy fans of Chauncey Schaffer. Certainly Commissioner Newton showed scant sympathy with the latter's survey of world events, regarding them as of little relevance to the case in hand.

Would the evidence have been considered strong enough to have led to the accused's arrest and trial had the murder been committed in New York instead of London? Newton felt obliged to answer yes.

And then, after delivering a tongue-in-cheek commendation of Schaffer's 'able' defence of his client – but pointedly refraining to comment on the line that the defence had followed – Commissioner Newton concluded:

'I wish it was in my power to discover any evidence or trace of innocence to justify me to withhold the certificate of extradition but I am free to say that, from all the combined circumstances, the chain which seems to have been linked around this man points fatally to him as the guilty man. So clear and distinct is the question of probable cause that I cannot for one moment have a doubt as to the proper course to pursue ...'

Muller, escorted by Tanner and Clarke, was put aboard the steamship *Etna* the following morning. She sailed for England five days later.

2

'Substantial Justice'

To quote the Duke of Wellington, in an entirely different context, it had been a near-run thing, though not even Tanner realised just how near. Certain elements in the English Press, stung by the abuse that was levelled at their country in the 'redbrick' republican newspapers, had begun to retaliate in kind, and had not the *Etna* sailed so soon after the court's proceedings, Muller might well have become the beneficiary of this Anglo-American slanging match.

Indeed, had he not been so impoverished at the time of his arrest, it is possible that he would have been placed on bail rather than confined in custody while awaiting the hearing of the extradition proceedings, and this in itself could have been fatal to the Yard's plans. With the Federal armies so badly in need of manpower, its recruiting agents were notoriously active at the courthouse door, and bail-jumping had become a patriotic virtue.

However, though Tanner and Clarke were still largely unaware of the factors that could complicate their apparently routine task, their suspect was even less informed and the journey passed off without incident.

The two detectives found Muller a rather puzzling prisoner. At a time when the extradition argument had raged its fiercest, and the tempers of defence and prosecution were at boiling point, the man whose life could depend upon the outcome had assumed the role of calm and almost disinterested spectator, seldom showing the slightest sign of discomposure or alarm. Now aboard ship, he preserved a similar detachment: polite and even pleasant to his warders, and displaying not the slightest trace of the violent disposition that could have been expected from one accused of so brutal a crime.

His sole request at the start of the voyage had been for something to read to break the monotony of being confined to his cabin. And, books being brought him, he had expressed his gratitude, taking particular pleasure in Dickens' *David Copperfield*. In fact, though the *Etna*'s journey was to last for twenty-three days, Muller gave not the slightest trouble to those around him, most of the excitement concerning the case, and his ultimate fate, emanating from sources nearer home.

Although the news of his arrest, conveyed to Greenock by fast steamer and thence telegraphed to 'Mr Reuter's office in Fleet Street', did not reach the British public until 6 September, the national newspapers had already given a coverage to Tanner's pursuit of the suspect that in latter days would have been sufficient to have jailed their editors for contempt and, possibly, defeated the whole object of the detectives' efforts by ruling out all prospects of a trial as 'prejudiced' from the start.

But following the report of the New York court proceedings, which arrived in England on the 13th, the discussion of the case in print had reached such disgraceful proportions that the *Daily Telegraph*, in belated repentance, had felt constrained to publish an editorial warning of the danger of forming a 'premature judgement'.

The main reason for this excessive publicity was undoubtedly the homely setting of the crime, providing as it did a largely train-travelling readership with a chilling sense of self-identification with its victim. But contributing almost equally to the public interest were the extraordinary ramifications the case had aroused abroad.

The United States had not been alone in being affronted by Westminster's contemporary foreign policy. Britain had also fallen out with her old ally Prussia over Bismarck's invasion of Denmark and the annexation of Schleswig-Holstein. Sensitive over the nationality of the accused, certain North German circles were now ponderously hinting that Muller was the victim of British spite.

By the time that the *Etna* dropped anchor off Queenstown on the evening of the 15th, the guilt or innocence of the young tailor looked like becoming an international *cause célèbre*. By the time that the steamer docked in Liverpool, twenty-four hours later, the German Legal Protection Society (Deutscher Rechtschutz Verein) had concluded arrangements for his defence. And to lead it they had chosen Sergeant Parry. At forty-eight, a genial and highly popular host to his fellow legal luminaries of the Temple, John Humffreys Parry, Serjeant at Law, was considered remarkable for the skill and resolution with which he would argue the cause of a client – however depressing its prospects – and his absolute failure to be intimidated or flustered. But now, as he broke the news that he had accepted the Muller brief, even the closest of the Serjeant's friends and admirers felt that his talents would be tested to the full.

The prisoner, still in Tanner's custody, had travelled down on the Saturday morning train, leaving Liverpool at nine and arriving in London at a quarter to three. The strength of public feeling against him was immediately made obvious by the crowds that had gathered outside Euston Station, and there were further demonstrations when he arrived at Bow Street, where he was duly charged and consigned to Holloway Prison to appear before the magistrates on the Monday.

In its choice of solicitor the German Legal Protection Society had done its subject proud. Thomas Beard was noted for the thoroughness and skill of his research, pursuing even the most obscure facts should he feel them to be of benefit to a client.

But speculation as to the line of argument that would be advanced for the defence, usually rife among lawyers on the eve of a major trial, was oddly muted. In fact, after the magisterial hearing of the formal evidence for the prosecution there were those who wondered how there could be any defence at all.

No one had testified to seeing Muller on the 9.50 on the night of the murder. No one had claimed to have seen him anywhere near the railway, whether at Fenchurch Street, Hackney or Bow. But even though the character and motive of Matthews, the principal Crown witness, had been under considerable attack, the weight of circumstantial evidence against the accused was so strong as to be considered overwhelming.

Certainly the coroner's jury at the resumed inquest on Mr Briggs had no difficulty in making up its collective mind when Muller was sent there between his appearances at Bow Street. It met at eight o' clock on the Monday morning. By ten it had returned its verdict: wilful murder by the accused. By eleven o'clock Franz Muller was before the Bow Street magistrate once more. By the end of the day he was committed for trial at the Old Bailey.

The machinery of the law, so often criticised as cumbersome and slow, had operated with almost startling speed and few saw anything in this novel departure from form that boded well for its prisoner.

As the day of the Old Bailey trial drew nearer the long odds offered to those few who gambled on the chance of an acquittal lengthened still

The trial of Franz Muller at Bow Street for the murder of Thomas Briggs.

further, until even the equitable Serjeant Parry must have experienced a qualm.

The defence team, in which his juniors were Messrs Metcalfe and Edward Besley, was strong; but the Crown team, headed by the Solicitor General, Sir Robert Porrett Collier, was even stronger.

Supporting Collier was Sir Hardinge Giffard, destined to take silk himself the following year and become three times Lord Chancellor; the redoubtable Serjeant Ballantine, noted for the aggressive thrust of his cross-examination in some of the most outstanding cases of the day, and Messrs Besley and Hannen, the latter recently the Attorney General's 'devil' and eventually, after heading the Parnell Commission, to become a Lord of Appeal.

'Overwhelming' though the circumstantial evidence might be against Franz Muller, the Crown had selected its advocates with care, all of them being worthy of Humffreys Parry's mettle.

At the commencement of the trial, on 27 October, the public benches in the Old Bailey's Court 1 were filled within minutes of their opening, and hundreds of would-be spectators had to be turned away. Private carriages as well as chartered omnibuses chocked the adjoining streets and extra police were employed to sort out the traffic jam. The pre-trial reportage expended by the Press, coupled with an unprecedented output from the ballad-mongers and pamphleteers, had assured Muller one of the biggest audiences ever to gather there. Indeed, so intense was the public's preoccupation with the trial that the Solicitor General, in opening the case for the prosecution, thought fit to warn the gentlemen of the jury that 'this is a case which has excited unusual and painful interest. It is one which, as we all know, has been canvassed in almost every newspaper. I might say in almost every house in the kingdom. And it is one on which some persons might be inclined already to form an opinion.'

And, as if to emphasise his desire to do justice to the prisoner, he added, with apparent sincerity: 'I must entreat you gentlemen, in approaching this most solemn inquiry, to discard from your minds anything that you may have read upon this subject.'

Understandably, this was a warning that Parry in his turn was later to stress with even greater eloquence and force, though hedged with doubts concerning its effectiveness. Indeed, as the Solicitor General summarised the evidence to come, it seemed to many in the court that even the most favourable Press comment could have done little to improve the lot of the accused.

And although much of the Crown case was already known to Humffreys Parry, it soon became plain that the prosecution had reserved for the trial some formidable surprises.

The hat that had been found in the railway carriage had, of course, already been stated to have strongly resembled the one that Matthews had purchased on Muller's behalf from Messrs Walker. But, since then, Walker's foreman had remembered that Muller's hat had been lined with a striped cloth identical with that which lined the exhibit. Yet their cloth had been in short supply a sample lot! – and only three or four hats, at the most, had been furnished with it.

More, it transpired that the hat found in Muller's possession on his arrival in New York had since been definitely identified as one made to the order of Mr Briggs' hatters, Messrs Dignance, by a jobbing hat-maker, who had pencilled in 'DD', the initials of the firm, to remind himself of its ultimate destination. But could this hat, which had found its way to Dignance, be shown to be the topper later worn by Mr Briggs? The prosecution argued that it could.

A shop assistant at the hatters was brought forward to testify that the banker had complained of the hat being 'a little too easy on the head', a fault that had been remedied by lining the crown with tissue paper. And shreds of tissue paper, found inside the hat, were produced by Collier and exhibited to the court.

Normally, the customer's name would also have appeared inside the crown, but as the crown had been cut down, and subsequently resewn, this did not apply. On the other hand, according to yet another prosecution witness, the resewing did not appear to have been done by a hatter. The stitches were of a type a tailor might employ.

And then had come the testimony of Briggs junior about the watch that Tanner and Clarke had extracted from the prisoner's bag. It was certainly his father's watch: he was sure of it, he stated. There was no possible way he could have been mistaken.

It was an impressive case, and held the court in rapt attention. It was also an apparently damning case: some felt that Muller's trial would be over that same day. Yet when Serjeant Parry rose to open the defence it was with no appearance of fluster or dismay. Instead, he opened with a grave and measured attack on the way in which the Press had handled the preliminaries to his client's ordeal.

The Solicitor General, he recalled, had invited the jury to discard from their minds all that they had heard, all that they had read, all that they had discussed about the case. 'But, gentlemen,' he said sternly 'this will be a difficult task.'

Articles had been written in the public Press proving that his client was guilty of murder. Articles had been written in the public Press proving that his client was not guilty of murder. And, while the writers in the Press had their own law of action, he considered it unusual 'that, when a man has been arrested upon a charge for which, if he is found guilty, his life must be sacrificed, not only the insignificant journals but the most respectable and most eminent papers of the country should have taken the course of commenting upon the likelihood of that person's guilt or innocence. Yet that has been done!'

It was certainly not the first time, nor would it be the last, that Humffreys Parry, confronted by prejudices, had acted on the maxim that the best form of defence was attack. But never before had he had to tackle a case about which prejudice existed on so massive a scale, or had been so extensively propagated by the sources to which the jurymen, in their everyday roles, looked to as the fount of information and guidance. For not only Grub Street, but Printing House Square as well, had tilted the scales against the accused, and only by haranguing on journalistic ethics had Parry felt able to establish even a partial counter-balance.

Now, after a performance well calculated to have made a conscientious jury feel guilt, or at least embarrassment, over prejudgements based upon printed hearsay, he commenced to draw attention to the one – but major – flaw in the prosecution's case: its evidence, impressive though it might sound, was entirely circumstantial.

Earlier, the Solicitor General, anticipating – and seeking to weaken – the defence's argument on this score, had reminded the jury that: 'It is by circumstantial evidence that great crimes are most frequently detected: murders are not committed in the presence of witnesses.'

But while piously expressing his 'entire concurrence' with this view, Parry now added the rider that 'if there be any doubt on that evidence when put before a jury, or anything that might cast a doubt on the evidence given, then the chain of evidence is incomplete and the jury ought not, and cannot, act upon it.'

There was, for instance, a vast difference between whether Muller ever had a hat like that found in the railway carriage and whether that hat really belonged to him: 'a difference as great as the difference between something and nothing, which is said to be infinite ...'

Furthermore, he reminded the jury, the main evidence presented against the accused in this respect had come from the cabman, George Matthews. Much, therefore, depended on the latter's veracity, and that veracity was a quality they might well discount.

Already the severity that had marked Beard's examination of the cabman in the magistrate's court had provoked Collier to protest that 'by the tenor of the questions, the defence is going to accuse Mr Matthew of the murder'.

Now, while denying this, though somewhat equivocally – 'dare I, with my finite and limited intelligence, affirm that which the Almighty alone knows' – Parry certainly made no bones about the fact that he was determined to destroy the cabman's credibility and portray him as 'solely actuated by a desire to obtain the reward'.

No body of sensible men would for a moment pay any attention to the evidence of such an unsatisfactory witness, the Sergeant continued, and then, ignoring further protests, he added daringly: 'I should be very sorry to charge him with being a party to the murder, but I should be very wrong if I were not to say that suspicion is pointing to him.' It had frequently been observed that Serjeant Parry was his brightest when a cause was at its darkest: in his handling of Muller's defence he positively glittered.

Matthews had told the jury that he had bought for Muller a hat exactly like his own, and much had been made of the fact that the accused could not produce that hat. But what had happened to Matthews' hat? At an earlier proceeding, when cross-examined by Mr Beard, witness had said he had recently disposed of it to a second-hand dealer, a Mr Downs, with a shop in Long Acre. A police check had revealed, however, that Downs had retired from business several months before. So what had Matthews done? He had changed his story, and said he did not know where the hat was; yet later had advanced the information that he had thrown it into the 'dusthole': curiously the very same thing that the witness, Mrs Repsch, had claimed that Muller had said to her when she had asked him what had happened to *his* hat!

And how trustworthy was Matthews in other respects? Scoffing at the cabman's explanation of why he had been so long in giving his story to the police, Parry said to the jury: 'Do you believe that he never heard of the murder before Thursday? I do not believe it. Murders, robberies and police cases of all kinds are the literature of cabmen. They read scarcely anything else.'

Witnesses waiting in the Old Bailey to be called.

Matthews' wife had known about the crime on Monday. The Repsches had known about it on Monday. 'And it seems almost impossible for me to believe that Matthews is telling you the truth when he says that he knew nothing whatever about this before Thursday.'

Next Parry reverted to the fact that Matthews, when under cross-examination, had at first denied – until pressed – that he had once been found guilty of a criminal offence. In the event this turned out to be for a 'trumpery theft' dating back thirteen years or so to the time when he had been a young ostler for a stage-coach company, and it had seemed rather unfair to have resurrected it. But, unrepentant, Parry said that 'though most reluctant' he had touched upon the matter to see what answer the man would give, and sure enough 'he had told a deliberate falsehood'.

It was a brave defence, a fighting performance that was to be described as one of the most notable of the century. Even the identity of the hat found in Muller's belongings – the hat claimed to be that of Mr Briggs – was challenged by the defence.

The hat had indeed been sold by Messrs Dignance, but Dignance himself was not prepared to swear that he was certain it was the one he had sold to Mr Briggs. 'And if Mr Dignance will not swear to it, will you by your verdict undertake to swear it?' asked Parry.

And, as for the supposed clue of the 'tissue paper' discovered inside the hat, Parry argued that – as defence witnesses would show – tissue was often used to line hats that got into the second-hand market, habitually a major source of supply for his impecunious client.

Even the fact that the watch found in Muller's possession had been proved to be that of the murdered man failed to unduly depress this devoted advocate. Nor was the fact that Muller had lied when he had told the detectives that he had bought it two years before allowed to pass without plausible explanation. The accused had since claimed to have bought both watch and chain from a man he had met when visiting the docks to book his passage.

'If', said Parry 'he purchased this watch and chain at the docks then there can be no doubt whatever that he would get them at an inferior price, and he must have known that he was committing a suspicious act. But it does not follow that he knew anything about the murder.'

Muller had indeed lied when he told Detective Sergeant Clarke that he had had the watch for two years, but if the jury considered the matter for a moment they would see that, irrespective of the murder, he had reason to believe that, in buying the watch and chain in such circumstances, he had done something that could lead him into trouble.

The prosecution had also made much of the fact that the Repsches had said the accused had been wearing dark trousers when he had left them on the Saturday prior to the murder but had been wearing light trousers when they had seen him again on the Monday – the insinuation being that the dark trousers would have been stained by Mr Briggs' blood.

This Parry dismissed as 'an inference that would not be drawn, I think, except in the mind of one who was determined to find something wrong in everything'. Matthews had said that the prisoner had been wearing a pair of dark trousers when he had met him on the Monday. Which of these witnesses was the jury to believe?

And in response to the alternative prosecution argument that, whatever the colour of the trousers he had worn on the night of the murder, Muller had failed to produce them, the Sergeant observed: 'There is one curious quality about Muller that will have been noticed. He is always either buying waistcoats or hats, making and pledging trousers or pawning watches. He was always doing these things. So what right has the Solicitor General to ask where are those trousers now? He has no more right to ask than the greatest stranger.'

Again, the prosecution had spoken of his client as a 'fugitive from justice', which was utterly untrue. For two months previously Muller had been expressing his intention of going to the United States. All his friends knew about it. He had told them all about it. He had booked a passage under his own name; he had pledged his pledges under his own name. 'Did the jury not believe that a man who had committed such a heinous murder only the preceding Saturday night would not at all events have used a false name?' Parry asked.

The address by Humffreys Parry to the jury lasted for precisely two and a half hours, its author sustaining himself with occasional sips of water. It was an exercise in persuasion that few other men could have equalled and also served to air a serious complaint that – too late for Muller – was to lead to a revolutionary change in the legal practices governing the conduct of a murder trial.

A defending counsel in a murder case was denied the right, which existed in the trial of lesser crimes, of addressing the jury at the end of the court's proceedings. The prosecution had the last word. The Serjeant, like several others of his profession, had long considered this unfair to the accused and now confided as much to the jurymen.

'If this were a case of a £10 note, if it were a bill of exchange, if it were a case of goods exchanged or sold, of work done, or if it were a miserable squabble between a hackney cab and a dust cart, I should be permitted to sum up the evidence for the defence,' he said. 'But this is simply a case of life or death and the law of England forbids this to be done. I feel very strongly on this subject.'

However, having made this point, and wryly accepting that 'we are in a court of justice, and not in a court of legislature', he startled his audience with the news that he intended to produce for the defence not only Mr Lee, that 'respectable gentleman' who had testified at the inquest that two other men had been present with Mr Briggs in the railway carriage, but would also bring forward an alibi to prove that Muller could not possibly have caught the 9.50.

It was in an atmosphere of intense drama that the court was adjourned until the following day. A similar atmosphere characterised the opening of the third day of its proceedings, Saturday 29 November. What had until then appeared to the average reader of the newspapers to be a clear-cut case of guilt had been transformed by Parry's skill. He had raised strong presumptions of doubt in the minds of the general public; but how far would his new evidence succeed in convincing judge and jury?

'A most respectable gentleman of independent means' was the way the defence had described their first witness, Thomas Lee. Unfortunately, it was his esteem for this 'respectability', coupled with an acute concern for the provision of his 'means', that made him, when in the witness box, a broken reed.

Lee's story that he had exchanged a good night with Mr Briggs when the train stopped at Bow, and then observed there were two other men in the banker's carriage at the time, aroused quite a stir among the public benches. So too did his admission that he did not feel that either of them resembled Muller.

But the gentleman's credibility took a hard knock once he was exposed to questioning, with Collier stressing his long delay before giving information to the police. Lee had claimed to be on friendly terms with Mr Briggs. Why then had he not come forward earlier? The Solicitor General was not the only person in the court to regard his failure to give evidence, until pressed, as 'very remarkable'.

But what really discredited Lee's character and, perhaps perversely, the value of his testimony as well, was when, having argued unconvincingly that he had not thought that it would be of 'much importance', he was provoked under further questioning to blurt out 'I had something else to do'. The son of a wealthy coal merchant, he had inherited considerable property and, as he explained with some hauteur: 'I had to collect my rents.' He had felt it a 'bother' to be involved in the case.

By the time that this most embarrassing of witnesses left the box, it was noticeable that even Parry's composure had slipped a little, though he regained it as he introduced what the Press was to describe as 'the Camberwell Alibi'. Yet here the effect of the evidence was dulled by the jury's view concerning the reliability of the witness. For although Muller's 'sweetheart', Mary Ann Eldred, was a pretty young woman, and of amiable disposition, she was also, in the parlance of the day, a 'fallen woman' – a freelance prostitute – a fact that the prosecution was able to employ to good advantage.

Miss Eldred lodged with a girl of the same profession at the home of Mr and Mrs Jones in James Street, Camberwell. Both she and the Joneses had been interviewed on Muller's return from the United States by a representative of the German aid committee and the solicitor Beard.

At first they had been startled to hear that Mary's 'little Frenchman', as they called him, was the Muller they had read about, accused of murder. He had always gone by the name of Miller when visiting the house and, like the Blyths, they had always regarded him as an inoffensive and likeable young man, a fact that must certainly have set him apart from the majority of Miss Eldred's demanding clients. In fact, it would appear that an affection had grown up between the two and that Muller, hinting expansively at his plans to visit the United States, had even gone so far as to ask the girl to go with him.

But when told of his story that he had been visiting her at the time of the Briggs murder, and asked if she could confirm this, Miss Eldred understandably could not be sure. Only by what Parry called a 'wonderful coincidence' was her memory jogged as to the sequence of events on that fateful night, a coincidence involving the arrival of a telegram. This, sent by a client anxious to reserve her services for the following day, had been received by her on a Saturday afternoon.

She had then 'gone out' for the night, as was her custom, only to be told by Mrs Jones the next morning that her 'friend' had called in her absence. At first she had thought that the landlady meant that the client who had sent her the telegram had arrived before his time, but then Mrs Jones had explained that by 'friend' she had meant' the little Frenchman'. He had called shortly after she had left – just after 9pm – and had stayed chatting with the Joneses for a while before leaving to catch the omnibus home.

It was weeks later, when trying desperately to remember the events of 19 July, in order to confirm whether Muller had visited her that night, that Miss Eldred had suddenly recalled this slight misunderstanding, and realised immediately that the telegram could provide a vital clue. Now a triumphant Parry was able to tell the court that the telegram had been traded and checked; and the date it had been sent was – Saturday July 19!

So the 'wonderful coincidence' had lived up to its name, or so it seemed: for if the Joneses' evidence was correct about the timing of Muller's visit, he could not possibly have got back to Fenchurch Street in time to catch the 9.50.

And then, to give additional support to Muller's account of his movements, the defence produced a bus conductor, Charles Foreman. In the course of the evidence for the prosecution it had been stated that Muller had injured his foot a few days before the murder and had taken to wearing a slipper when he walked abroad. Now, out of the blue, Foreman testified that he had carried a passenger from Camberwell Gate who had worn a single slipper. He remembered this because, a sufferer from gout, he had reflected at the time that the traveller 'had a touch of my old complaint'. It was the last trip of the night and the bus did not reach King William Street until 10.20 – thirty minutes after the train carrying Mr Briggs had left Fenchurch Street, and about the time of the discovery of his body.

All the same, though Parry rightly emphasised that 'a passenger in an omnibus with a carpet slipper is a very rare kind of passenger' he had to confess that Foreman, on seeing Muller in custody, had been unable to identify him positively as that passenger, and the jury had to be content with the 'hope that, on examining him, more may come to his recollection'.

Unfortunately for the defence this 'hope' failed to materialise, for under cross-questioning Foreman admitted that, although positive the incident occurred in summer, 'I can't say whether it was in July or August'. As a result, his evidence was considered worthless, and he was dismissed from the case.

So on what testimony was the defence basing its hopes and arguments? According to Collier, on little more substantial than 'the clock of a brothel, the keeper of the house, and the statement of one of the unfortunate women who resided there'.

It had been said of the Solicitor General that the sleeves of his black silken gown concealed the claws of a tiger, however immaculately manicured. In the Muller case he did justice to that description. The cross-examination of Eldred and the Joneses was pressed aggressively and ruthlessly, with small mercy given to their 'unfortunate' mode of livelihood. And, beneath his sharp questioning, the 'alibi' began to look every moment less secure.

How could they be so sure about the vital point of that alibi – the time of the accused's arrival and departure from their house – when eight weeks had passed since then? And how was it that, when first approached by Beard they had failed to say anything about the 'telegram alibi'?

Although, to quote the subsequent comments of the Lord High Baron, Mary Eldred was listened to by the court with 'attention and compassion', it was obvious that the prosecution's repeated references to her trade was doing much to discredit her value as a witness. It was equally obvious that, even though she stuck to her story, the Joneses themselves were frightened and confused – as well they might be – by Collier's sarcastic innuendoes as to their background. Even the fact that Mrs Jones used a different surname from that of her current husband – she had married twice – was given a disreputable significance.

Seldom can Parry have had so much reason to regret the legal process that deprived him of the right to address the jury again and to redirect their minds towards his arguments. But it was when Collier, at the end of the day, arose to avail himself of the privilege denied his opponent, and make the final address before the judge's summing-up, that the most damage was inflicted on Muller's cause.

Although some of the Solicitor General's insinuations, when seen in cold print and divorced from the emotion-charged setting in which they were placed, may seem today to have had an odd – even morally dubious – look about them, there was no doubt that they had a great impact on the jury.

'A more unsatisfactory and more dangerous alibi has never been set up in a Court of Justice', Collier solemnly, if inaccurately, informed his audience. All that the defence could 'set up' against the evidence on behalf of the Crown was the reliability or otherwise of this 'brothel clock'.

It was fortunate, perhaps, for the man who led the prosecution that no one thought fit to ask him how many inmates were required for a house to classify as a 'brothel', or just why a clock should be less reliable when functioning on the mantelpiece of a 'brothel' than when installed in a more respectable environment.

The point about Collier's repeated jibe was that Mrs Jones had stated that Muller must have called at the house around 9.30 because she remembered that she had looked at the kitchen clock about half an hour earlier and, finding it was then nine, had called to Eldred that it was time for her to go on her rounds. And the girl herself, though frankly confessing she did not recall this specific incident, had told the court that she was in the habit of 'going out' just after nine each night – 'except on Sundays!' – and that it would have been natural enough for the landlady to have drawn her attention to the time.

But Collier would have none of it. With withering side references to the goings-on in this particular household, and pouring scorn both upon the accuracy of Mrs Jones' memory and the punctuality with which Eldred pursued her dubious employment, he asked the Jury: Do you suppose that the proceedings of this respectable and well-conducted establishment are regulated like clockwork?' The idea, he exclaimed, was preposterous.

Yet as Parry might have argued – had he been free to do so – it was the very imprecision of Mrs Jones' evidence that, in this instance, gave it its strongest claim to authenticity. For had she, as implied by the prosecution, sought to bear false witness in Muller's favour, then surely she would have claimed that she had looked at the clock at the time of the man's arrival? And surely she would have asserted that the clock hands had then stood at precisely 9.30, rather than have timed his call by guesswork about the period following Miss Eldred's departure? But on this and similar matters of relevance, the defence had to remain silent.

The picture that the Solicitor General presented to the jury had a vastly different colouring from that produced by Humffreys Parry, and left the Camberwell alibi looking distinctly tattered. It was based on the assumption that Muller had left the Repsches' at the time they said he had – at a quarter to eight – and thus would have arrived at 'this woman's' house no later than half past eight, or at the latest, a quarter to nine. Then, with a fine disregard of the fact that the Repsches' clock might have been as unreliable in its time-keeping as the Jones', Collier commenced to elect on this somewhat slender base a veritable mountain of theory.

'He calls at this woman's house', he said, with a sudden dramatic switch to present tense, 'but he does not stay above a few minutes. There is nothing to stay for, because the girl is out. So he goes back, and takes the omnibus that will carry him to London Bridge – and, if he starts at about a quarter past nine, he will have arrived at King William Street just about the same time that Mr Briggs would arrive there.

'And what would be the station the accused would then go to in order to travel to the place where he lived? Why, Hackney Wick station, sometimes called the Victoria Park – and he would be going home by the same train as Mr Briggs. Gentlemen', concluded Collier, 'I cannot but think that this is a most dangerous alibi.'

At 4pm the Lord Chief Baron, Sir Frederick Pollock, sitting with Mr Baron Martin, began to deliver his charge to the jury. It was an address that could make all the difference to their verdict and Muller knew it. Rigid and pale-faced he stared straight ahead of him at the bench, as if mesmerised by the sword of Justice secured to the wall above the judge's bewigged head.

Sir Frederick was then eighty years old. According to a *Times* obituary notice, which appeared seven years later, he was 'kind, gentle and courteous. At the Muller trial his emphatic eloquence moved the deepest feelings of his audience'. It was an eloquence, however, that was to move them against the prisoner.

While ostensibly agreeing with the prosecution on the importance of circumstantial evidence, Parry had argued that this applied only when 'there is no link wanting in the chain'. The Lord High Baron was quick to take up this point and then, with due courtesy, knock it down again.

The watch, the chain, the hat that Mr Briggs lost on the night of his murder, and the hat that was found in the carriage in place of his, these indeed were links of the same chain, he told the jury.

'But do not make the mistake which it appears to me that Serjeant Parry is rather inclined to lead you into, that if one link of that chain is broken you have got rid of the prosecution.' There were three separate and distinct links, he pointed out, each of them having a separate history, and a failure on the part of one did not in the slightest degree affect the position of the others.

It had been said of the Lord Chief Baron that 'his leaning was ever to the side of substantial justice rather than to mere technical accuracy'. From the nature of his address at the end of the Muller trial, it was evident that the weight of circumstantial evidence against the prisoner had decided him as to the type of verdict by which 'substantial justice' would be best served.

Like Collier before him, he gave short shrift to the defence testimony put forward by Thomas Lee: 'Whether Mr Briggs was seen at Bow with another person or not I will not say. Lee, who was there, and did not consider it his duty to make a statement respecting what he saw is, I think, scarcely in that frame of mind which is deserving approbation.'

And he went on to add: 'If indeed the prosecution had known what Lee had to say in examination and cross-examination, I am not surprised that they did not call him, and they did quite right not to call him.'

The alibi on which the defence had fixed so many of its hopes was dismissed with equal brevity.

'Between seven and eight o'clock', said Sir Frederick, 'the prisoner was at Repsch's. He then left, taking his boots with him, saying he was going to Camberwell. There was plenty of time for him to have gone to Camberwell, and then return.'

This was surely a conclusion that many a Londoner, subjected to the vagaries of the transport of the day, would have had cause to consider unduly optimistic: certainly it was not supported by any positive analysis. Yet it was allowed to pass without any challenge, attaining the authority of a statement of fact.

Even Parry's criticism of the Press's pre-trial coverage of the murder – as likely to influence the jurors against his client – was treated as of little importance by the judge. Indeed, he appeared to make a virtue of the circumstances whereby, because of the newspapers, 'you have come to the inquiry with your minds furnished with certain facts which are an essential part of the question, and I think you are better able to enter into the matter than if you had come here as entire strangers to all the circumstances'. Fair statements – 'I abstain from saying discussions' – appeared to be one of the benefits of the Press that he would not desire to see curtailed.

It was left to the German Legal Protection Society, in pursuit of their subsequent appeal against the sentence passed on their countryman, to point out that the 'discussions' concerning Muller's guilt or otherwise had occupied many pages of print on both sides of the Atlantic; a development over which certain prominent journals had themselves expressed unease.

Although summarily dismissed by the Home Secretary of the day, the Society's complaint that Muller had been condemned by public opinion long before he came to trial would seem to have had a considerable basis of fact.

It was 3pm when the twelve good men and true of the jury filed out of the tall wooden pew that flanked the dock and withdrew to consider their verdict. But although the twin, glass gas globes suspended over the long table in the centre of the retiring-room had been lit lest the

Mr Baron Martin passes sentence on Muller.

jury's deliberations should be overtaken by the fall of darkness, they were absent from the court for only fifteen minutes and, as they stood up to answer their names, it was noticeable that they avoided looking towards the prisoner. The silence that greeted them was so intense that the scratch of the clerk's quill pen seemed an almost indecent intrusion on the court's solemnity, as much a trespass as a ribald song in church.

Yet even before the Clerk of Arraigns began to put his formal question to the jury – 'How do you find the prisoner at the bar? Guilty or Not Guilty?' – practically every person in the crowded court had realised just what the answer would be. Only the slightest of murmurs greeted the foreman as, rising from his seat, and still averting his eyes from the accused, he pronounced the verdict: Guilty.

And all that remained was for Mr Baron Martin, placing the black cap on his head, briefly to announce his approbation of the verdict, tell Muller that 'I wish to remove from your mind any hope of an alteration of sentence', and conclude with the grisly direction that:

'You be taken from here to the prison whence you came, that from thence you be taken to your place of execution, that there you be hanged by the neck till your body be dead, that your body when dead be taken down, and that it be buried within the precincts of the prison where you were confined. And may God have mercy on your soul.'

3

Excursion to Horror

The first man to be convicted of murder on the railway, Muller had two other dubious claims to fame: as the originator of a hat that became a fashion – Winston Churchill was one of its devotees – and as one of the last of the melancholy and miscellaneous throng of unfortunates condemned to provide for the nation's entertainment by being hanged in public.

Just fourteen years before Muller met his fate, some railway companies in the North of England had enterprisingly arranged cheap excursion trains to carry sightseers – from all available points – to the hanging of Gleeson Wilson, who had murdered a family of four. Nor were the promoters disappointed in the fruits of their gamble. Of the hundred thousand men, women and children who crammed the Liverpool streets to witness the spectacle, it was said that a good fifth had come into the city by train.

A rail excursion with a similar object occurred in the same year in what is now the British Rail Eastern Region, when the dissolute and wealthy bucks of the Swell Mob chartered a special train to Norwich. There, suitably supported by a cargo of champagne, they aimed to join in the fun that would accompany the hanging of James Rush, tenant farmer, who had shot dead his landlord and his landlord's son, and seriously wounded the latter's wife and a maidservant.

In this instance, however, the Norfolk police – fearing that the activities of these visiting 'gentlemen' would serve only to increase the anticipated disorders – stopped the train at a wayside halt and, disregarding all protests, packed them off home.

An 1867 satirical sketch of a public hanging.

After all, there was plenty of entertainment for them back in London.

'I believe a *public* execution', Charles Dickens wrote to a friend, 'to be a savage horror behind the time.' But although in 1856 a Select Committee of the House of Commons unanimously recommended that such spectacles be ended, and that the condemned should be hanged inside the prisons that housed them, the Lords, with due regard both for the 'corrective effect' of public hangings upon potential wrongdoers, and the maintenance of a cherished national tradition, opposed the move and succeeded in blocking it.

In this, their lordships enjoyed not only the plaudits of those who looked to such occasions to augment the profits of their trade – ranging from rail magnates to ballad-mongers and Punch and Judy showmen – but also the righteous support of a large section of the church and chapel community, convinced that sin should be followed by public expiation. Yet – and some might consider the circumstance ironic – the most emphatic approval for the Upper House in its defiance of the elected chamber, came from the broad mass of London's poor.

In the metropolis the enthusiasm of the mob for public hangings had by no means abated since the abolition in 1783 of the procession of condemned felons from Newgate Prison to Tyburn, nearly adjacent to the site of the future Marble Arch. On the contrary, the new location of the gallows outside Newgate Prison made it even more convenient for the bulk of the spectators – the teeming populace of the City, riverside Southwark and the slums of the East End.

To such as these, any hanging was a sort of carnival, but Muller's hanging was an attraction that drew in thousands more, among them many members of what, in the parlance of the day, was described as 'the better class'.

For people who relied on the railways to carry them daily to counting house and chambers from districts as far afield as Enfield, Anerley and Croydon, it was the very familiarity with the setting of the crime that had aroused their interest in the execution of the criminal.

That fatal night I was determined,
Poor Thomas Briggs to rob and slay
And in the fatal railway carriage,
That night, I took his life away.
His crimson gore did stain the carriage.
I threw him from the same, alack!
I on the railway left him bleeding,
I robbed him of his watch and hat.

Doggerel it might be, but the 'Lamentation of Franz Muller' was not only a best-seller among artisans and serving girls, it also gave rise to uneasy reflections in a thousand or more comfortable villas in the suburbs.

I never thought the law would take me,
When I sailed o'er the raging main
All my courage did foresake me,
A murderer in the railway train ...

Among train travellers throughout the country the fate of poor Mr Briggs had an intensely personal significance, arousing the frightening thought 'It could have been me!'

'This,' as Parry had put it to the jury, 'is a crime which strikes at the lives of millions. It is a crime which affects the life of every man who travels upon the great iron ways of this country' ... a crime of a

Condemnation of FRANZ MULLER.

FAREWELL hope—all is despair!
No hope is left the murderer here :
Flight could not the murderer save,
Although he crossed the briny wave.
The brand of Cain was on his brow,
The past cannot be recalled now ;
Nothing now his life can save,
Muller is doomed to a murderer's grave.

Nothing on earth Muller's life can save,
From the scaffold and a murderer's grave
All escape for him has failed,
Even the ship could scarcely sail ;
Long days and nights of anguish led,
Always in fear, always in dread.
With blood-stained hands the blows were
        given,
He could not cast his eyes to Heaven ;
His innocence he still out-braved,
Yet Muller found a murderer's grave.

His aged victim looks from Heaven,
Prays for his murderer to be forgiven ;
Hurried from the world of woe,
In the midst of health, by that fatal blow.
By one so young, you'd scarce believe,
His artful ways could so deceive,
But the eye of God he could not brave,
Sentence of death and a murderer's grave

Mothers may weep for their children dear
But who for Muller will shed a tear ?
Perhaps far from friends and far from
        home,
In a loathsome cell, in anguish mourn.
Dark visions, perhaps, surround his bed.
In misery rests his weary head,
The love of gold made him its slave,
And brought him to a murderer's grave.

The sentence, Death, to him is given,
Prepare your soul for a place in Heaven,
Three weeks to live—how time will fly,
On the scaffold, Muller must die.
The time is given for him to live,
Is more than he gave to Mr. Briggs.
He is with angels, led by each hand,
Yet before Heaven's judgment Muller
        must stand.

Yes, he must suffer for his crime,
A young man scarcely in his prime ;
A few months back perhaps he was good,
His conscience free, on his soul no blood,
No one knows how his fate's decreed,
Perhaps to make our hearts to bleed,
Let us hope his soul he'll try to save,—
Pray for a murderer when in his grave.

H. DISLEY, Printer, 57, High Street, St. Giles, London

Contemporary poem: 'The condemnation of Franz Muller'.

character to arouse in the human breast an almost instinctive spirit of vengeance.'

That spirit, accompanied by others even more destructive, was to rule unchecked in London streets on Monday 14 November.
'Yesterday morning Muller was hanged in front of Newgate. He died before such a concourse as we hope may never be assembled, either for the spectacle which they had in view or gratification of such lawless ruffianism as yesterday found its scope around the gallows.'

Thus the correspondent of *The Times*, oppressed, as well he might have been, by the recollections of his assignment only ten minutes walk away from Printing House Square.

The preparations for the crowds expected for Muller's execution had begun the preceding Friday, when structures resembling in purpose the crush-barriers today employed on happier functions, were erected in all the streets that led directly to Newgate. Bodies of police patrolled the area, to clear the gangs of vagrants and other undesirables whom even this sign of industry could be expected to attract. Other officers rehearsed methods of protecting the more prosperous visitors from the attentions of the garotteers, 'bonneteers' and pickpockets to whom such excellent soil presaged a bumper harvest.

All through the night, and on the Saturday, the top-hatted, heavy-handed 'Peelers' continued to clash with various groups, although, as *The Times* observed the following day, 'these were not composed of the real regular *habitués* of the gallows, but mere young beginners, whose immature tastes were satisfied with catcalls in the dark, fondling the barriers, or at most a hurried, scrambling throw of dirt at the police when they dispersed them'.

It was on Sunday night when the real business began. The motley collection of loungers and drunks who had endured with patience the prevailing drizzle had moved on by 11pm leaving the regular execution crowd to take their places. *The Times* recorded:

A thick dark noisy fringe of men and women settled like bees around the nearest barriers and gradually obliterated their close white lines from view. It was a clear bright moonlit night. Yet though all could see, and well be seen, it was impossible to tell who formed the staple part of this crowd that gathered there so early. There were well-dressed and ill-dressed, old men and lads, women and girls. Many had jars of beer; at least half were smoking, and the lighting of fusees was constant, though not more constant than the cries and laughter as all who lit them sent them whirling and blazing over the heads into the thicker crowd behind. Occasionally, as the rain, which fell heavily at intervals, came down very fast, there was a thinning of the fringe about the beams, but on the whole they stood it very steadily, and formed a thick dark ridge round the enclosure kept before the Debtors' door where Muller was to die.

And, centre of all eyes – 'or at least of very many of them' – was the solitary gleam of light that, emerging from a single window above the black bulk of the prison wall marked the spot, 'that very spot' where Muller rested: the condemned cell.

All through the dismal dark hours, and despite heavy showers of rain, the crowd continued to grow. At 3am someone in the fringe of the mass that had formed a sort of quadrangle around the place where the scaffold was due to be erected, attempted to preach, but his voice was soon drowned by a bedlam of groans and laughter. A little later another man began the old familiar hymn of 'The Promised Land'. A few joined in, but this effort too was quickly silenced when the mob began to bawl such topical ditties as 'Oh My, Think I've Got to Die' and 'Muller, Muller, He's the Man', the latter composed and published before the trial had even begun. However, even these choral offerings, punctuated by the screams of those who, hemmed in by the multitude, were the victims of robbery and assault, were soon terminated.

It was a dull rumbling sound, familiar to every connoisseur of the hangman's craft, that caused the songsters to pause, and then convert their efforts into shouts, hisses, handclaps and delirious cheers. Drawn by cart horses, appropriately black, the timber paraphernalia of the gallows was trundling up to the prison walls and was now given its traditional reception. All that had passed so far had been a drawn-out prelude to the opening act of the play. Now the audience could relax and enjoy itself. And what an audience!

To quote once more that eloquent reporter from *The Times*:

As every minute the day broke more and more clear the crowd could be seen in all the horrible reality in which it had been heard through the long wet night. All the wide space in front of Newgate was packed with the masses inside the barriers, and kept swaying to and fro in little patches, while beyond these again, out to St Sepulchre's and down towards Ludgate Hill, the mob had gathered and was gathering fast. Among the throng were very few women; and even these were generally of the lowest and poorest class, and almost as abandoned in behaviour as their few better-dressed exceptions. The rest of the crowd was as a rule made up of young men, but such young men as only such a scene could bring together – sharpers, thieves, gamblers, betting men, the outsiders of the boxing ring, bricklayers, labourers, dock workmen, German artisans and sugar bakers with a fair sprinkling of what may be called as low a grade as any of the worst there met – the rakings of the cheap singing halls and billiard rooms, the fast young 'gents' of London.

But all, whether young or old, seemed to know nothing, fear nothing, to have no object but the gallows, and to laugh, curse or shout as, in this heaving and struggling forward, they gained or lost in their strong efforts to get nearer to where Muller was to die. Far up, even into Smithfield, the keen, white faces rose rank above rank, till even where the houses were shrouded in the thick mist of the early dawn, the course of streets could be traced by the gleam of the faces alone, and all, from first to last, from nearest to furthest, were clamouring, shouting, and struggling with each other to get as near the gibbet as the steaming mass of human beings before them would allow ...

By eight o clock the police estimated that the crowd had increased to fifty thousand and that this figure related only to those in the immediate vicinity of the prison. On the fringes there were many thousands more.

Asked if he had anything to say after sentence had been pronounced on him by Baron Martin, Muller had told the court that, while 'satisfied' with his judges and with the jury, he had been convicted on false evidence, and not a true statement. 'If the sentence is carried out I shall die innocent'.

Throughout his fortnight's stay in the condemned cell he had maintained this attitude. Even now while Calcroft, the hangman, busied himself on the preliminaries of his calling, the young German showed no sign of either fear or remorse. He was pale and composed.

The thick stone walls of the Press room of Newgate Prison reduced to the faintest of whispers the roar of the crowd that awaited him, and his immediate audience was small. Save for the abjurations of Dr Cappel, a Lutheran minister provided by the German Legal Aid Society, they were also completely silent.

At that time it was the custom for selected representatives of the Press to be admitted to the prison, to observe the behaviour of the condemned and witness his execution. In Muller's case, the three so favoured were Peter Sarlsby of *The Times*, Gerald Potter of *The Globe* and a Mr Clyatt, who was to represent the rest of the newspapers, national and provincial.

The exterior of Newgate in the 1850s.

Sketches inside Newgate Prison, the condemned cell.

But (surprise, surprise!) Mr Potter it transpired was not at all enthusiastic about this journalistic plum, and Fred Wicks, a young sub-editor of *The Globe*, volunteered to take his place. Many years later, in a letter to the *Sporting Times*, Wicks was to explain: 'I felt my education would not be complete without having seen a hanging ...'

There were times, however, when he was to repent this enlightened zeal for learning: times such as when Calcroft, the pinioning completed, left the room to check his preparations of the scaffold.

'It was at that time', Wicks recalled, 'that I felt as if a little more callousness would have served me well. To be a passive spectator at such a scene is not a sedative. The imagination will not leave the bare neck and the pinioned arms. One thinks of the hangman examining his rope and the hinges and bolts, and one feels a terribly eerie feeling creeping over one.'

To bolster his sagging morale, he had recourse to what he described as an 'odd expedient'. He ate a piece of biscuit, and found that 'this distraction carried me over the horrid interval, which was made all the more impressive by the constant tolling of the bell of St Sepulchre's Church'.

In fact, when Calcroft reappeared to lead Muller, accompanied by the minister, up the flight of steps that led to the scaffold, it was probably the strength derived from that solitary biscuit that enabled our diligent journalist to sustain his search for truth and overcome his distaste sufficiently to follow at the trio's heels.

It occurred to him that perhaps Mr Jonas, the governor of Newgate, might not take too kindly to his appearance on the platform and regard it as an unnecessary intrusion, 'but nothing seemed to me to be more proper, and I was well repaid for my temerity. I SAW THE PEOPLE'.

The spectacle with which Wicks was confronted as he reached his privileged perch was quite extraordinary and – biscuit or no – would appear to have overwhelmed him, though only temporarily, with its ugliness.

'Far as the eye could reach,' he told his readers, 'over to Ludgate Hill on the one hand, and right away to Holborn on the other, the entire space, broad and distant though it was, presented an unbroken mass of human faces - types of every unholy passion that humanity is capable of – a seeing sea of hideous brutality that had been surging over the space the live-long night, and was now almost still with expectation.'

And he went on to record that: 'The mouths of the myriad of grimy yellow faces were open, and all the thousands of eyes were upturned upon the spot where I stood, with an intentness that was more appalling to me than the methodical movements of Calcroft and the unimpassioned attitude of Muller. The contrast was marvellous ...'

For a man who was still perfecting his education in his calling, Wicks would seem to have had an excellent – and dispassionate – eye for detail, plus a remarkable capacity to dismiss what in weaker colleagues would have been a mounting nausea. He would also appear to have been blessed by a pen sharp enough to record each one of the hangman's actions: 'He passed a strap round Muller's legs and buckled it; he put the rope round Muller's neck and tightened the slip knot just under his right ear; he slipped a noose at the other end of the rope over an iron hook depending from the crossbeam of the scaffold. And last of all he pulled a dirty yellow bag over the man's head to his chin. He then stood aside.'

All through these macabre proceedings, the prisoner had maintained the same unimpassioned manner that had characterised him at his arrest and trial. According to *The Times* correspondent he appeared 'quiet and self possessed', and had undergone the process of pinioning with 'unfaltering courage'. Now, as Dr Cappel once more addressed him, and Calcroft ominously disappeared from view, the diligent *Globe* man noted that the minister seemed the more excitable of the pair, even though the prisoner was standing on the drop.

'In a few moments you will stand before God,' said Dr Cappel. 'I ask you again, and for the last time, are you innocent of this crime?'

Muller answered: 'I am innocent.'

'You are innocent?' the minister queried.

'Yes, I am innocent. God knows what I have done.'

For the conscientious Cappel the moment must have been one of the almost unbearable tension. As he later confided in a letter to *The Times* he had developed a deep compassion for Muller and had determined to 'strengthen him for eternity' though he had never believed in his complete innocence, however resolute his denial of the murder charge. Thus when, an hour and a half before the time set for the execution, his young German countryman had suddenly called on him to remain with him to the last, the pastor had concluded he had determined to make a confession. Yet now, only minutes from eternity, he was still persisting in his refusal to own his guilt and Cappel was besieged by terrible doubt. Could it be that justice had been mistaken and would hang an innocent man? Or that, if not, his charge was to die unrepentant?

'God knows what you have done,' he worriedly persisted. 'But does he also know if you have committed this crime?'

There was the slightest of slight pauses, and then came the sudden, unexpected answer. 'I have done it.'

No sooner were the words out than the trap fell.

Calcroft had done his work well. One convulsion and all was over.

But even before the crowd, its brief silence ended, broke into a roar of profane exultation and surged towards the jail, Dr Cappel had vacated the scaffold. Dr Cappel was almost delirious with relief.

Rushing down the stairs with his hands aloft, he was shouting to the officials as he ran: 'Confessed! Confessed, thank God!'

Nor did the pastor's excitement wane when, seated in a chair in the Press room to recover his breath, he was accosted by those who, less dedicated than he, and less venturesome than Wicks, had chosen to witness the execution from the prison itself. In the next ten minutes he told them three times over the gist of that memorable conversation on the scaffold, his eyes moist with ardour as he did so. A brand had been plucked from the burning.

The end of Franz Muller had come suddenly. So suddenly that many were later to claim that his last words, spoken in German, were ambiguous and, far from being an admission of guilt, could have been a profession of innocence, cut short by the hangman's well-greased trap and rope. But to the only man who had heard those words distinctly their import was unassailable, and was to remain so until the end of his days. Muller had confessed.

Moved by the representations of the German Legal Protection Society and disturbed by the preconceived bias that had been so evident during the trial, the editor of *The Times* had made vigorous efforts on the condemned man's behalf, and Cappel, on the morning after the execution, not only expressed 'the thanks of every friend of humanity for those efforts' but also described the 'confession' and the events leading up to it.

'The persistency of Muller in his previous denials was probably owing to his strong love of life', the Pastor wrote, 'and his seeming frankness partly explains itself by the supposition – of which I am firmly convinced – that no murder had been intended, but that the robbery led to the death of the victim.'

Coming from the one source to have established a close rapport with Muller throughout his imprisonment, it was a theory that, whatever the element of doubt attending his confession, appeared to many thinking people to make considerable sense. But even among those who differed from this view and argued that the crime had been perpetrated with foresight and the intent to kill, there was widespread concern about the scenes that had preceded and followed his execution.

'None but those who looked down upon the awful crowd of yesterday will ever believe in the wholesale, open broadcast manner in which garrotting and highway robbery were carried on,' *The Times* recorded. And, loudly echoing this condemnation of 'the lowest refuse of metropolitan life', other newspapers found no shortage of outrages with which to chill their readers' blood.

In fact, it was because of the public alarm over the activities of the thieves and cut-throats who had imposed their rule upon the crowded streets during Muller's hanging, rather than any great revulsion at the hanging spectacle itself, that now gave fresh strength and courage to those who so far had argued in vain the case for reform.

In 1868, following the recommendations of yet another Royal Commission, the Capital Punishments Amendment Act was passed. From then on executions were conducted in private.

The Muller trial was by no means the first occasion when the judiciary had felt it salutary to comment on the hazards that could – and did – beset the lone traveller by rail. The little tailor had secured for himself a position in the gloomy pantheon of villains that was unique inasmuch as he was the first murderer to have chosen a railway carriage as the setting for his crime. But he was far from unique in having seen in the privacy afforded by the heavily curtained corridorless compartments towed by the Iron Horse a golden opportunity for profitable violence.

A case that attracted much attention in the 1850s involved the unhappy experience of a young teacher who, travelling from Rochdale, was attacked by a passenger who pressed a revolver to his head, knocked him out, poured liquid chloroform into his mouth as he started to recover, and robbed him of his money and watch.

Captured and brought before that same Judge Martin who was later to pronounce the death sentence upon Muller, the culprit was awarded the maximum punishment for his crime, six years' hard labour.

'It would be frightful indeed,' said the judge, 'if men are to escape from the severest penalty of the law for cases of such a character as this. For, should they so escape, then no man will be safe when travelling in railway carriages.'

And, even before this direful judicial prophecy, an American visitor had complained to the *Derby Mercury*: 'I am not a timid man but I never enter an English railway carriage without having in my pocket a loaded revolver. How am I to know that my travelling companion may be a madman escaped from confinement or a runaway criminal? And what protection have I against their assault, if it should please them to attack me, but the weapon I carry?'

It is fair to add that such extremes of precaution, sensible though they might seem to a mere foreigner, were seldom adopted by the natives, usually more concerned – until Muller's crime aroused them – with the ghastly discomforts and high accident rate of contemporary rail travel than with the opportunities it offered to the criminal.

The murder of Thomas Briggs created, as we have seen, an extraordinary alarm among the public, and particularly did this apply to the commuting middle classes.

As Matthew Arnold, a regular traveller by the Great Eastern Railway from Woodford, Essex, to the City was to sardonically recall: 'The demoralisation of our class caused by the Bow Street Tragedy was complete.' Himself a transcendentalist, Arnold escaped the infection, and delighted each day to ply his fellow passengers with all the consolations that his philosophy suggested.

'I reminded them how Caesar refused to take precautions against assassination because life was not worth having at the price of an ignoble solicitude for it. I reminded them what insignificant atoms we all are in the life of the world.'

Not surprisingly, he found this of no avail. 'Nothing could moderate in the bosom of the great English middle class their passionate, absorbing, almost bloodthirsty clinging to life.'

And another contemporary observed of the general reaction that it was extreme enough to give holders of rail stock 'nightmares of apprehension.'

Nor was murder the only theme of fear that, taken up by the Press was to be echoed in Parliament. If a man could be killed by one type of villain, then might not a lone lady's virginity be taken by another? Setting shapely limbs to tremble beneath crinoline and bodice was terror of rape.

It was in an effort to allay such bad-for-business fears and abate the storm of parliamentary criticism that otherwise might bring unwelcome legislation in its wake, that the board of the prosperous and progressive South Western Railway decided at an emergency meeting to install small portholes in the wooden walls that divided the compartments in the company's corridorless carriages. But this move, widely advertised at its inception as 'a boon to the unaccompanied traveller of either sex', was not so well received as its enterprising sponsors had expected.

Protests were soon being made by those its purpose was principally to protect: namely, the ladies. The portholes – christened 'Muller's Lights'– made travel intolerable, they claimed, because of the attentions of peeping Toms.

Well, something had to be done to reassure the public but, as the company's directors quickly realised, the 'lights' were obviously not the answer, even though they were to survive on country lines for another twenty years until the existing rolling stock wore out. Nor did another innovation, sliding panels, fare much better. The need, as the Press insisted, was for 'a method of communication' between passengers and train crew. Deciding what form that method should take was far more complicated.

Four years after the murder of Thomas Briggs the public pressure on the railway companies still showed no signs of slackening, and it was a measure of the seriousness with which they regarded the climate of opinion that the rivals agreed to a then unprecedented step. At a special conference they decided to pool their resources of expertise and form a joint committee to examine the crop of suggestions and inventions – sensible and insane – by which they had been bombarded from almost the day after the unfortunate widower's passing. But, at the end of their cogitations, the committee found themselves to be in agreement only on the desirability of an 'alarm' system: opinions still differed widely on the type of system to adopt.

To the enterprising directors of the London and South Western Railway Company, and its neighbour and rival the South Eastern, the invention submitted by a Mr Preece was the favoured instrument: one that was described as 'simple in the extreme, and consisting merely of a strong clever adaptation of that power of the future, Electricity'.

The Preece 'apparatus' was housed under glass in each compartment and – in theory – all the passenger had to do to call for help was to break the glass and pull at the ring beneath it. This would then cause two semaphore arms, projecting from the outside of the carriage, to fall, clash together, complete a circuit and set alarm bells ringing in both the guard's van and the engine cab.

But despite the LSWR's enthusiasm for this venture into technology, other companies – distrustful of the claims made on behalf of so new-fangled a device – plumped for an alternative that, if less spectacular, would, they felt, be more easily 'understandable' to the passenger in its working, and also, by coincidence, less exacting on their pockets.

Stripped of all superlatives, this majority choice consisted simply of a rope that stretched from front to rear of the train, with a bell connected to it at each end. A tug on the rope would set both bells ringing, causing the driver to apply his brakes as prelude to the railway staff combining for a 'rescue'.

Confused by this disagreement between experts, the government – introducing the Railway Act 1868 for parliamentary approval – hesitated in committing itself to the choice of either. Instead, it settled for a measure enjoining each separate company 'to provide and maintain in good Working Order in every Train worked by it which carries Passengers and travels more than Twenty miles without stopping, such efficient Means of Communication between the Passengers and Servants of the Company in charge of the Train as the Board of Trade may approve.' And with equal tact the board 'approved' both systems.

Alas for the folly of human expectations. Although the Press, reflecting the confidence of the companies, looked forward to the new devices as heralding an era 'when the traveller of either sex can journey without apprehension of attack', the systems that had worked so well under test conditions proved all too fallible when exposed to the rugged realities of the Victorian permanent way.

Soot and grease prevented Mr Preece's 'electrical marvel' from functioning more than spasmodically, and seldom when it was needed. And the 'simple' rope installation – though enriching the English language with 'communication cord' – became at times almost intolerably complicated, billowing outward and going slack when the train rounded curves at speed.

The introduction of the American Pullman car to Britain in 1874 with its long saloon interior promised relief to the female traveller of the perils to which her sex exposed her by providing surroundings 'where she can be free of all fear of insult', but initially Pullman was used only on the Midland Railway, the rest of the companies still employing carriages with individual compartments and no corridor along which an accosted lady might flee, or other passengers advance towards her rescue.

In general, the only way of escape from a would-be ravisher was via the carriage door or window with death the most probable alternative to dishonour, unless of course, the victim could succeed in balancing on the outside of the train and climbing into a neighbouring compartment – a hazardous acrobatic feat that only the most nimble could accomplish.

One who did so was a certain Miss X travelling alone in a first-class carriage on the South Western. Miss X's ordeal began when she was accosted by the dashing Colonel Valentine Baker of the 11th Hussars, who joined the train at Liphook. At first flattered by the military gentleman's attentions, this well brought up young woman was horrified when he revealed his real intentions – 'base', she described them later – and resisted him strongly as he kissed and embraced her. Then, all pleas to desist proving of no avail, she managed to break free and pull the communication cord. It did not work. Finally, in desperation, she threw open the door, jumped on to the wooden running board, and stayed there for five minutes until fellow passengers, hearing her screams, succeeded in pulling her into a neighbouring compartment.

Miss X's assailant, arrested at Waterloo, was subsequently sentenced to a year's imprisonment and discharged from the army in disgrace. For his shocking lapse of behaviour, so unbecoming an officer and gentleman, Baker was later to make honourable amends by going into exile, taking service with a foreign power, rising to the rank of general and dying bravely in the field.

The directors of the South Western confessed to having been a little over-confident in their valuation of the company's emergency stop arrangements.

Communication cord or 'electric marvel' notwithstanding, the predicament of the virtuous Miss X, and others like her, had demonstrated all too clearly that the victim of a physical assault could never rely with certainty on summoning even the slightest attention to her plight, let alone conjure up immediate rescue. In fact, as was to be shown in a bloody tragedy enacted on the Brighton line, both train staff and passengers could be deaf even to pistol shots.

4

Murder in the Dark

Just a few seconds after the 2.10pm from London Bridge to Brighton – her whistle wailing like a soul on the way to Hades – had plunged from out of the scorching sunshine and into the icy blackness of the Merstham Tunnel the shots were fired. At the time, however, no one recorded them as such.

Guard Walters was later to explain that he had heard two loud reports but had assumed they came from fog detonators on the track – an odd assumption on that bright summer's afternoon, with the temperature outside the tunnel in the eighties.

To William Gibson, a Brighton chemist, the 'explosions' were four in all, and were sufficiently noisy to upset his small son, already apprehensive of the sudden dark of the tunnel. Although comforting the boy by saying 'don't be frightened, they're only fog signals', the chemist, unlike Walters, had his doubts.

Passengers in another third-class coach were also to recall hearing 'a number of bangs', but these had made little impression on them at the time. As the train had continued at speed they had felt that all was well.

And as for the fireman and driver – well a cannon shot would have been needed to penetrate the hearing mechanisms of Messrs Smith and Fulgrove. Beset by the roar of escaping steam, the coming together of the iron footplates and the clanging of the shovel against the sliding coal, they were deaf to all but the clamour of their environment. 'We never heard a thing,' they were subsequently to tell the coroner.

Contemporary sketch of the Brighton Terminus.

Not until thirty minutes had gone by and the train pulled up at its scheduled stop at Preston Park, just short of the Brighton terminal, did its passengers realise that there had been an attempt at violent crime. But even then they had no idea that they had been travelling in the company of murder.

It had long been the custom of the London, Brighton & South Coast Railway to collect the tickets of its main-line passengers at Preston Park, a mile short of Brighton Station, rather than at the terminal itself. On the afternoon of 27 June 1881 – a Monday – Collector Gibson had good reason to wish for an exception to the rule. For no sooner had the semi-fast train from London come to a stop than he was confronted by a dazed and near hysterical young man, stumbling from a first-class compartment in the second coach behind the engine, and pointing frantically as he did so to the open door behind him.

His shirt and jacket were drenched with blood. Blood also was encrusted on his hair and forehead. And there was blood even on the visiting card that he produced when Gibson, after a quick horrified

New saloon carriage on the London, Brighon & South Coast Railway, 1873.

74

look inside the compartment, asked his name. 'Arthur Lefroy of 4 Cathcart Road, Wallington, Carshalton. Author and journalist.'

It was a strange and chilling tale the traveller excitedly unfolded. There were two other men in the compartment – so he said when he entered it at London Bridge. One of them was a prosperous-looking gentleman in his late fifties while the other was a rough-looking bewhiskered character, 'probably a countryman'. Neither had spoken to him, or to each other, and the journey had been without incident – until the train had entered Merstham Tunnel. Then, suddenly, he heard a loud report, and received at the same time a violent blow on the head. After that he remembered nothing until, recovering consciousness, he found himself lying on the floor, bleeding profusely and quite alone. Both his companions had vanished.

Gibson took another look at the carriage. There were patches of blood on the walls, door and seat cushions. There was also blood on the displaced foot-rug, and every sign of there having been a desperate struggle. He called the station-master, a Mr Hall.

The latter listened to this startling story, which by then had been considerably improved upon. No longer 'remembering nothing' Lefroy said that he had been attacked by the countryman. He had been hit on the head and shot. But Hall, though impressed by his apparently wretched condition, had been quick to put into words the puzzle that had been occupying the collector. Just where were these fellow travellers? The 2.10 had made only one stop, at Croydon, and the alleged attack had occurred several miles further south. So if Lefroy really had been the victim of an assault, just how had his assailants managed to escape?

Lefroy mumbled that they could have made their way to another carriage. But no one, as Gibson testified, had passed through the ticket barrier at Preston Park. Nor was there anyone still aboard the train who answered the description he had given. Again, to judge by his own condition, the clothes of the attackers would have been heavily blood-stained.

Perhaps then, it was suggested, they had 'got out on to the way' from the carriage when the train was still in motion? It was a possible solution, but highly improbable. Average speed on the semi-fast was over thirty miles an hour.

Hall now examined the carriage: scattered on the floor were several 'flash sovereigns'. Pocket-pieces minted in Hanover, these were practically worthless in terms of cash, but used as counters in card games. They were also in great demand among characters anxious to 'impress'. Lefroy, however, claimed he knew nothing of the pieces and suggested that they must have belonged to his attacker. He had not been robbed, he said; his property was accounted for.

But, even as he spoke, the station-master noticed something protruding from the passenger's left boot. He looked again, scarcely crediting what he had seen, and then asked, 'Sir, why are you carrying a watch and chain in the side of your boot?'

Momentarily Lefroy appeared a little embarrassed, but his answer came pat enough. Being of a nervous disposition, he explained, he was in the habit of concealing anything he had of any value before boarding the train, this a precaution that had proved, in the present instance, to have been all to the good. But still Hall continued to wonder.

He finally decided to send the injured man to Mr Anscombe, the Brighton station-master, with a request that the latter arrange for a medical examination. But he also decided to send him in the 'care' of Gibson and another railway worker, both of whom were instructed not to part from him until not only Anscombe had seen him, but also the railway police.

A gangling, extremely skinny figure of a man in a shabby genteel frockcoat, and perhaps, because of his thinness, looking taller than his modest 5ft 8in, Lefroy struck Collector Gibson as a rum sort of fellow, very prone to changes of mood.

At first almost deranged, or so it seemed, by his dreadful experience, he had perked up surprisingly quickly and had appeared to be enjoying the attention the event had focused on him, his air of self-importance increasing by the minute. Yet now he seemed put out that the railway authorities should be taking the matter so seriously. Only grudgingly had he agreed to report to the police.

Again, although professedly so shocked by the attack, he was evidently composed enough to care about his appearance. He had lost his collar and tie, which presumably had been torn from him by his assailants, and his first question concerned where he could obtain replacements for them. Furthermore, he had then insisted on being taken direct to the place recommended, a small shop in James Street, close to Brighton Station.

But if Gibson was puzzled by the behaviour of his charge, so too were the railway police, called in by Anscombe to probe his story and displaying a reaction that was anything but sympathetic. These two passengers the man had talked about, just where had they gone? Did they exist in fact, or was the whole incident fiction, a figment of a disordered imagination? And while orders were issued to search the track for trespassers, or their bodies, another very different sort of search was also instituted – a search of Lefroy's own person.

Carried out in defiance of his protests, this yielded little that was relevant to the proof, or otherwise, of his tale. A pocket book, a quantity of coloured tickets – 'the latter having the appearance of those small printed cards employed by betting men at the races' – and, of course, the watch and chain, by then transferred from boot to pocket, were found upon him. But his objections to this procedure, rather pompously expressed, were ignored completely by his two interrogators.

Indeed, it was only after they had asked him why he was visiting Brighton, and he had answered a trifle haughtily that he had come down from London with the express intention of discussing with Mrs Nye Chart a play he had written for production in her theatre, that police attitudes towards the newcomer began to change.

Manageress of the prestigious Theatre Royal and Opera House, Mrs Chart was a well-known figure locally and possessed of much influence. By association, Lefroy must be influential too. The temperature thawed. Suspicions eased. And, as if to confirm still further his respectability and sincere concern, the injured man came up with the offer of a generous reward for his assailant's capture.

By the time Lefroy was taken to the County Hospital to have his wounds attended to, the railway police had largely been won over to his story. Nor did the results of the subsequent medical examination do much to disillusion them. While confessing that he had never before seen 'anything like' the marks on his patient's face and hands, surgeon Bernard Hall thought it possible that six small semicircular cuts upon his scalp could have been caused by 'a pistol or revolver pressed against Lefroy's head'. And the 'wild-eyed' appearance of the man – the doctor conceded that at first sight he had thought him insane – could have been because his wounds were 'sufficient to produce fantasies'.

The hospital visit gave to Lefroy's account of the attacks a vastly increased credibility. So too – and this was to prove ironic – had the discovery of two revolver bullets, one of them in the seat cushions and one wedged into the woodwork near the communication cord, or as the LBSCR preferred to describe it, the electric communicator. The 'loud report' Lefroy had claimed to have heard could have been the sound of a shot that had narrowly missed him!

Not until much later did critics of the initial police handling of the case wonder why no surprise had been registered when he then insisted that he return to London forthwith. He had urgent and pressing business awaiting him in London he claimed when the doctor suggested he was in no fit state to travel. Yet no one bothered to point out that he had left London only an hour and a half before. Nor did anyone query why he had bought only a *single* ticket.

And how long had he expected his interview with Mrs Chart to have lasted if he was now so anxious to leave the town? And Mrs Chart herself, what had she to say about the credentials of the so-called playwright? Later, this failure of the police to make inquiry of Mrs Chart was to be described as 'curious'.

All the same, however much impressed by Lefroy's apparent harmlessness, the railway police were not altogether heedless of the desirability of keeping track of his future movements. And so, regardless of his protestations that he was now fully recovered and could fend for himself, they insisted that, as a matter of 'routine courtesy', he should be escorted on his journey home.

Thus, when he boarded the train for London, he was in the company of Detective Sergeant George Holmes, an officer of eleven years' service in the Metropolitan force who had been seconded, as was the custom, to the London, Brighton & South Coast Railway to augment the modest numbers of the company's own police staff.

As the two settled in their compartment on the 6.10pm from Brighton, the coach in which Lefroy had allegedly suffered his ordeal was being examined in a neighbouring siding. News of the police investigation had spread and the team checking it for clues were surrounded by gawking sightseers. Meanwhile, however, some thirty miles up the track, platelayer ganger Thomas Jennings was gazing at an even more grisly scene.

'Select your terminals, and run your line between them as straight as you can.' Such had been the advice offered by that amateur, but far-sighted enthusiast, the Reverend F. S. Williams, back in 1852, a boom year for railway development. In his monumental work *Our Iron Roads*, a classic of the pioneering period, he had stressed that it was not even necessary to have a single house along the route between those terminals.

'Open the line', he wrote, 'and as people once flocked to the banks of that first great highway, a river, so will they flock to your railway too.'

Alone among its contemporaries, the London, Brighton & South Coast Railway had high hopes of this prophecy coming true. Moreover, it had made the clergyman's formula company policy and had spared no expense in the process of carrying it out.

With stage-coach running times so much improved that the road journey between Brighton and London had been reduced to only four hours, the LBSCR had little margin for the rambling detours to serve secondary towns and even villages that were demanded, and provided elsewhere. Instead, it drove straight for its objective, taking the shortest possible route, and flattening – or burrowing through – every natural obstacle.

It was in one of the costliest by-products of this adventurous progress – the mile-long Balcombe Tunnel – that a discovery made by Ganger Jennings, inspecting the line in company wit his nephew William, gave both men their claim to fame. But few on that warm day in 1881 would have envied them the nature of their find or the eeriness of its setting.

The Victorian traveller had a horror of railway tunnels that was intense, deep planted and very largely justified. Originally: it had been freely forecast by the anti-railway lobby, mistrusting the Iron Horse and its voracious appetite, that asphyxia would over take those daring to venture into those smoke-filled catacombs, and even when this prediction proved groundless, fears of sickness from 'the foul air smoke and sulphur' still survived to haunt the timid for decades' afterwards. As a medical journal of the period put it: 'The deafening peal of thunder, the sudden immersion in gloom, and the clash of reverberated sounds in a confused space, combine to produce a momentary shudder, or idea of destruction, a thrill of annihilation ...'

Less fanciful, however, was the widespread fear of the consequences of an engine failure in a tunnel, when, because of the shortcomings of the signalling system, there was always the chance of a collision. And since the 1860s and the publicity afforded to the Muller case, ever present was the dread of assault or even murder in the darkness.

However, to the Jennings', the Balcombe was no monster but just another of their several places of work. Both of them were railwaymen, as were all the other males in the family. Ever since Tom's father had foresaken the green Sussex fields for the Iron Way's more lucrative employment, they had made the railway their vocation and, as professionals, had scorned the fears of laymen, even though – as they wryly conceded – more of their kind were killed by accidents in tunnel work than in any other branch of the service.

In fact, as they entered the Balcombe's echoing blackness Tom and William's first sensation was one of relief. Outside the rails were shimmering in a heat haze, and the work gang's naked torsos were running with sweat. In the tunnel it was cooler than the coolest of larders. It was at 4.30 that their feelings abruptly changed. Caught in the glare of Tom's naphtha light was what at first seemed to be a shapeless pile of clothes lumped in the six-foot way dividing the up track from the down. But as he moved towards it he found to his horror that a disarrayed jacket concealed a bloodied and battered face, upturned to the tunnel's ceiling. The body of an elderly man lay at his feet, his right arm flung across his chest as if to ward off a blow. His left fist was dug into the ballast. Around his neck was a broken gold watch-chain.

'What's up?' It was young William's voice and Tom did not immediately answer. Instead, he pointed wordlessly at the body. 'Should we move him?' The boy's words came hesitantly and after a long silence. ' Tom Jennings, recovering, shook his head. 'No sense in that' he said. 'The feller's dead.'

After one more look the two turned back the way they had come, hurrying towards the pale glow that marked the tunnel's entrance.

It was platelayer Stephen Williams who, informed by Tom Jennings of his grisly find, had hastened to alert the Balcombe signal box, from which the message had been telegraphed to London. But there had been some delay before permission was granted for London Bridge to transmit the signal to other stations along the line, and even when this was done there was a curious omission.

Three Bridges, Haywards Heath and Croydon – in fact all stations north of Preston Park – were duly alerted, yet Brighton, southern HQ of the company's police, was kept completely ignorant of this startling sequel to Lefroy's attack story. Otherwise, most assuredly, the 6.10 would have been short of two of its passengers.

Over ninety minutes had passed since Jennings' discovery of the body, but neither the detective nor his charge knew anything of this when the train pulled out of Brighton Station, and Lefroy was in a voluble and apparently cheerful mood as he related yet again the exciting events of his journey down.

It was not until the train stopped at Balcombe and the stationmaster of Three Bridges Station, a man called Brown, entered the compartment, that Holmes received the first intimation that Lefroy's oft-reiterated tale of outrage could be other than it seemed.

Keeping his voice low, Brown told him of the body found on the track, and also passed on to him a warning not to lose sight of Lefroy, a warning that, in view of the circumstances, might well have been considered superfluous, yet instead proved merely to have been a wasted effort. Although the exact sequence of what followed is somewhat obscure, and made the more so by the widely-differing Press accounts published – shades of the Muller case! – long before the evidence offered at the trial, what is transparently clear is that the policeman was certainly no match for the man he was escorting. Lefroy had him out-manoeuvred from the start.

To quote one of his ex-colleagues writing to the *Daily Telegraph*: 'Lefroy had a habit of ingratiating himself that was remarkable, and in conversation possessed a power of narrative that was essentially dramatic, not to say sensational. In the presence of strangers he was polite and respectful, and his general bearing was such as to produce a favourable impression.'

It would appear that, in his dealings with Holmes, he deployed these persuasive talents to the full. They were talents that were to cost the Detective Sergeant dear.

> At Wallington perhaps the most important event has been the completion of the sewerage scheme, so far as this village is concerned, for which the ratepayers are having to pay, and will for the next thirty years have to pay, so heavily. Whether the scheme was a wise one is a question which it is useless now to discuss ...

Although the editor of *Pile's Directory* for 1882 gave the sewerage scheme pride of place in his chronicle of the 'village's' progress through the preceding year, a close runner-up was the programme of 'improvement' to the local railway station. Having noted approvingly that 'the rows of houses in South Beddington and in Wallington bid fair soon to join in forming one continuous forest of buildings', the directory added that 'the facilities offered by the railway company add to the eligibility of the village for residential purposes'.

A sewerage scheme ... additions to the railway station ... and on the next page an account of the excitement that followed the vicar's revelation that the parish was short of funds for its church school and might have to endure the 'infliction' of a school board ... It was with distaste that *Pile's*, turning from these topics of legitimate concern, reluctantly reverted to the affair that, only a few months earlier, had so disturbed the tranquil sense of wellbeing enjoyed by this respectable community, projecting its name so prominently into the public prints. The writer confessed:

> It may be thought that we have neglected a duty if some reference is not made to what has been known world-wide as the Brighton murder

case. So nauseous has been the conduct of the daily Press on the matter, that we feel no inclination to dwell on it. Wallington, probably, has attained more notoriety during the past six months than it has enjoyed during the whole of its previous existence, and for ourselves we should be content if it were never to attain it again; at any rate on the same grounds.

And, this said, he was at pains to point out:

The connection which the village had with the murder was that the murderer resided in it for two years with some relations, and that he made his escape from it on the night the crime was committed. In no other way was it connected with the crime and we, therefore, must ask to be excused from referring to it any further. If any of our readers desire to know more on the subject they must refer to the daily papers for the past six months, and unless they happen to be of extraordinarily morbid temperament, we can safely say that they will be sick of the subject before they wade through all the verbiage which has been written.

Sick of the subject? Mrs Clayton, for one, would have shared the directory's sentiments on the matter. In the archives of the Lefroy case this lady and her husband are but shadowy and insubstantial figures of no real relevance to the defence or prosecution, and featuring purely by reason of the fact that the accused, a remote relative, lodged with them. Yet innocent though they were of the affair, the subsequent tittle-tattle was to have for the Claytons the most humiliating consequences, driving them from their home and out of the district altogether.

However, on the night when Lefroy, with Holmes in his wake, came home unexpectedly early to the house in Cathcart Road where Mrs Clayton ran what was to be extravagantly labelled by the Press as an 'academy for young ladies' – in reality a nursery for a handful of tiny tots – the sole concern of the couple was for their lodger's state of health. From the moment he had first called on them three months before, and Mrs Clayton had shown her sense of family by agreeing to take him as paying guest, they had never quite known what to make of 'Arthur'. He was unpredictable: full of fine optimism and cheerful talk at one moment, but completely down in the dumps a moment later.

He 'wrote' for a living, it was understood, though they did not see much of his writing. He also boasted a strong attachment to the boards, and indeed there was even talk of his presently producing a play. When he spoke of the leading stage personalities of the day he referred casually to them by their Christian names as if they were on familiar terms, and he hinted too of rich patrons in the City. But baffled though they were by his pretentions, the Claytons were fond of him and, it would seem, rather proud of him as well. Not every Wallingtonian could boast a genius in the family.

Thus, when the bandaged Lefroy had made his appearance, the couple were full of pity and concern that he should have been the victim of an apparently unprovoked attack. And, having believed implicitly in his account of that affair – for what reasons had they to doubt it? – it followed that they also believed his explanation of the presence of the policeman. Holmes, he explained, was acting as his bodyguard, to make sure he came to no harm before he produced his evidence to Scotland Yard! Neither the Claytons nor the detective at that stage were to know of the latest development in the drama that was being enacted on the railway line between the Merstham and Balcombe tunnels.

While Lefroy continued with his 'preparations' – which were to prove of a very different type from those he had pretended – and Holmes continued to wait restively in the hall for his reappearance, the body discovered by Jennings four hours earlier was being identified as that of a retired Brighton merchant, a Mr Gold, and the Clayton's 'genius' relative was being connected with his murder.

It had been a long and troubled shift for Thomas Jennings. Accompanied by his brother and his brother's son he had helped escort the dead Mr Gold to the Railway Inn in Balcombe village, a good mile to the north of where they had found him. And then, in the company of a PC he had gone back to search the tunnel. There they found two bronze coins: 'flash sovereigns' minted in Hanover and similar to those that had been in the possession of Lefroy.

The face of the dead man had been covered by a blanket when they had placed the body on a stretcher, and for that Tom Jennings had been duly grateful, for what had happened to Gold's face was sufficient to move even the hardest case to nausea. It was black with the dirt of the footway between the tracks, but also had the appearance of being scorched by explosive powder from a shot fired at point-blank range. A semi-circular wound disfigured the mouth, extending from one side of the chin to the other, and was encrusted with congealed blood. This, so it appeared, had been caused by the point of a knife, and there were other knife wounds in the cheeks and hands.

There were fourteen such cuts in all, and also a wound three inches in length in the back of the head, open down to the bone. Called in to

Scenes from the Lefroy murder: 1. a room in the cottage from which two men were seen struggling in a railway carriage; 2. train passing the cottages at Horley; 3. the entrance to the Balcombe Tunnel; 4. the spot in the tunnel where Mr Gold's body was found; 5. Cathcart Road, Wallington, where Lefroy lodged.

inspect the corpse, a local doctor reported that death had resulted from haemorrhage, and this in turn had been the effect of a violent blow delivered by a blunt instrument or, perhaps, from the dead man's fall from the train. Tom Jennings was not the only member of the track party to be glad to be spared a close-up view of the injuries that had given rise to such coldly clinical appraisals.

Around the neck of the deceased was a gold watch-chain, to which was attached an eye-glass and two highly polished pennies. But the chain had been broken short and there was no sign of a watch. It could well have been torn from him in the course of a violent struggle.

Poor Mr Gold. What sort of a man had he been? His clothes though 'sensible', were of good quality and before his blood had soaked them must have been worth a bob or two. And who had he left behind to mourn his violent passing? Or rejoice, as the case might be, over a handsome inheritance. It was nearly midnight before the landlord of the Railway Inn got an answer to the questions with which his regulars, and a local Pressman, had persistently pestered him: and even then, the answer was incomplete.

The last train from London usually passed through Balcombe at high speed, causing the trees near the station platform to curtsy in its wake before slowing for its passage through the tunnel. But on the night of the 26th it made an unscheduled stop to release from a first-class carriage a middle-aged lady, 'handed down' with some reverence by a male companion, and wearing over her face a long black veil. The widow of the deceased had arrived.

Mrs Gold, it transpired, was in no state to view her husband's body, then lying in a small brick shed adjoining the inn itself, and had left the task of identification to a Mr James Hollis who had come along with her for that purpose. Nor was Hollis – visibly much shaken by his mission – in any sort of anecdotal mood.

All that could be gleaned from him was that Frederick Isaac Gold was a former stockbroker, a little more than sixty years of age. He had retired from business eighteen years before and, for the past ten years, had lived in Preston. He usually travelled to London on Monday mornings to attend to some investments he had made there, returning by the 2pm train, arriving at Preston Park at 3.30. And with that an inquisitive public had to be content.

But, while Hollis was discreetly fending off the laymen, the police were pursuing their own line of inquiry, and this concerned a matter in which only the distraught Mrs Gold could be of any help: namely, the make and appearance of her husband's missing watch.

It was a question they approached with some degree of diffidence for the widow was not only grief-stricken, but bitterly angry too. When her husband had failed to arrive home when expected, she had at first assumed he was detained on business, but by the time the 8.15 arrived, and there was still no sign of him, she had become so alarmed that she had walked down to Preston Station, to inquire if there had been an accident. Yet, rather oddly – in view of his previous encounter with Lefroy – the station-master had made light of her wifely fears and assured her that all was normal on the track.

Indeed it was not until ten o'clock that she had received a telegram from Balcombe acquainting her with the finding of her husband's body nearly six hours before, and the telegram had been delayed in delivery because of a slip-up by the Post Office.

Yet inspite of such distracting circumstances and the fact that she still had not been informed that her husband's death could be other than accidental, Mrs Gold – in her answers concerning, the watch – turned out to have an eye for detail that an analyst might envy. Not only was she about to give her interrogators a full description of the watch's appearance – gold, white-faced and with the name of its maker printed on its face – but she was also able to tell them that the watch-maker's name was Griffiths, with an address in the Mile End Road.

For the railway police this was a major clue and, in marked contrast to their previous proceedings, they wasted no time in following it up. If their hunch was correct, Mrs Gold's information could resolve immediately the mystery of her husband's death – revealing him as the victim of a murderous robber. A robber who had tucked his loot inside his boot!

Accordingly, the police in Croydon were asked to contact Holmes. He was to compare this detailed description of Mr Gold's watch with the watch Lefroy had claimed to be his own and, should the two tally, he was to put the man under arrest.

If ever a sleuth failed to live up to the expectations aroused by his auspicious sounding surname, it was the unfortunate Sergeant Holmes. At Croydon, from whence he and his charge had travelled by cab to Cathcart Road, a police telegram had been handed to him that stated that, as the body on the line bore a broken watch-chain, but was without a watch, he should obtain, and check on, the number of the watch in the possession of Lefroy.

But this he had postponed doing until, comfortably ensconced in the drawing-room, he had sent for pen and paper, and after a social chat with the Claytons, had asked his charge if he felt well enough to elaborate on his previous statement. In fact it was late – very late – when he got round to the question of the number, to be told that it was 56,312.

And even when, having opened the back of the watch he found this was not so, his reaction was remarkably slow. 'You have made a mistake', he told Lefroy. 'It's 16,261.'

'Yes, I forgot', the latter coolly answered.

At which, as he later testified at the trial, Holmes' sole move was to make a note of it. 'Having found the correct number,' he explained, 'I struck out 56,312, and put in 16,261.'

He next went to far as to ask Lefroy if he knew the maker's name. 'No,' came the answer, 'I bought the watch off a friend.' What friend? Who was he talking about? Incredibly, Holmes failed to inquire. Instead, he asked where he could be found next day, and was content to record the answer as 'Wallington, up to 12. After that at the United Arts Club, Savoy Street, Strand.'

All in all, it would appear to have been a courteous interview, terminating with Lefroy apologising for his fatigue after the excitements of the day, and insisting, as the detective took his leave, in accompanying him to the door.

Only when Holmes reached Wallington Station and received the second telegram, advising him of the make and number of Gold's watch, did he become even partly aware of the opportunity he had missed. Yet even then his moves were far from urgent.

Having got back to the house – a mere six minutes' walk away – he decided to stay outside, maintaining surveillance while awaiting the arrival of reinforcements. And when these arrived on the scene after another hour's delay, it was to discover that while Holmes' eagle eye had been trained on No 4's front door, the suspect had made a quiet exit by way of the basement and the servants' stairs leading up to the street. All that Lefroy had left behind him were the blood-stained trousers and grey overcoat he had been wearing when he had made his dramatic descent on Preston Park. And all that Holmes was left to contemplate was the ruin of his reputation.

A sad day for the police. A great day for the Press. Aggrievedly a spokesman for the Brighton police told the *Sussex News*: 'There seems to be a general impression in Brighton that the Borough police were responsible for allowing Lefroy to slip away at Wallington. It should, however, be borne in mind that it was the railway, and not the Borough police, who had charge of Lefroy when he escaped.'

Reacting even more strongly, Scotland Yard issued an immediate statement that publicly disclaimed all responsibility for Holmes' action – or lack of action – and described him as being on the staff of the LBSCR. In this the 'Met' was being more than a little devious. Holmes had merely been on loan to the railway company who paid his salary direct to Scotland Yard, a point that, in their turn, the directors of the company were quick to emphasise. And yet, while the unhappy Detective Sergeant was made the scapegoat for Lefroy's escape – his eleven years of service counting for nothing in face of the popular fury at the way in which he had been so singularly outsmarted – there were those who argued that part of the blame at least could be said to have lain at the door of his superiors.

Why, for example, had there been no check on the fugitive's initial reference to theatre-owner Mrs Chart? Only after Lefroy had left Brighton had that lady been interviewed, when she revealed that she had never heard of him. And why the uncritical acceptance – until several hours later – of his explanation that he had tucked the watch and chain into his boot in order to conceal them from thieves?

However, on the following Tuesday morning these shortcomings of the authorities were still largely unknown, and the main point of discussion around the breakfast tables of a public aroused for the second time in eighteen years to the vulnerability of railway passengers to murder, centred on the horrific injuries sustained by Mr Gold, and the failure of the 'Alarm Device' to have brought others to the rescue.

Nor did the company's subsequent explanation that the electric alarm apparatus had since been tested, and found to be in excellent working order, do much to allay the general feeling of insecurity. If Gold, when grappling with his attackers had been unable to pull the cord, then surely there should be a change in its location. On many a staid head of family, waiting at his local railway station that sunny June morning, the thought of the old gentleman's fate cast a most unseasonable gloom, arousing the uneasy reflection, 'There, but for the grace of God ...'

It was in the early afternoon that popular interest shifted from the fate of the murdered man to the identity of his murderer, a move brought about by the police notices beginning to appear in every public place.

Wanted for Murder. Arthur Mapleton, alias Lefroy – a reporter aged 22 ... height 5ft 5in, thin dark hair cut short, small dark whiskers; last seen at Wallington at half-past nine on the 27th (last night) with his head bandaged. He was dressed in a dark coat, and wore a low black hat; had scratches upon his throat, and was wounded, it is supposed by a pistol shot. He has a gold, open-faced watch, No. 16261, maker Griffiths of the Mile End Road.

The hunt was on!

5

An 'Expeditious' Hanging

'Murder. £200 reward.' It was on 4 July, a full week after Mr Gold had plunged – or been thrown – to his death beside the railway track, that Scotland Yard found it necessary to issue yet another wanted notice, and back it with what was, by the monetary values prevailing in the 1880s, a very handsome reward for information. However, only half of the £200 came from the Yard's resources. As in the Muller case, the balance was contributed by the railway. And meanwhile the police grip was tightening; everyone known to have had even the most tenuous association with the wanted man was subjected to questioning.

From the moment of their lodger's disappearance from their once tranquil and well-ordered villa, the Claytons had been major victims of this toughened policy, their daily routine being subject to frequent unwelcome surprises. The railway police, the local police, the detectives from Scotland Yard ... all had taken a turn in visiting and interrogating them, 'turning the place inside out as they did so', Mrs Clayton complained.

Nor had Lefroy's other relatives been spared such attentions. The day after publication of the first hue and cry, the wanted man's sister, a Mrs Brickwood, was interviewed at her home in Southend, while detectives searched the place from top to bottom. But although, as in Cathcart Road, their search for the suspect proved fruitless, they found that the lady had much to say that was relevant regarding his character and background and, in addition, the strange state of his mind.

The last she had seen of her brother was at Christmas, when he had called on her with the news that he was about to drop the family name of Mapleton, and use only the second name, Lefroy. He had boasted that he was going to write for the stage, and the latter name sounded more 'select' and was easier on the ear.

For similar reasons he had abandoned Percy as his Christian name and had adopted that of Arthur instead. Mrs Brickwood also confided that in her opinion this 'mere boy', as she described him, was not always fully responsible for his actions; in fact, she could never really understand him. His grandfather had died insane, and his father, at the time of Percy's birth, was suffering from softening of the brain.

So much for Mrs Clayton's 'genius' seen through the eyes of his sister. All the same, it was evident that his sister still had some degree of affection for him. Vain and unstable though his behaviour might be, he also had good qualities, she said. And generosity was one of them. To help her out of a temporary difficulty for a few months earlier, he had sent her part of £50 he had received on attaining his majority. For the detectives this conversation was an illuminating one, though not everyone would have agreed with Mrs Brickwood's opinion of Lefroy's benevolence.

One of the first to respond to the police appeal for information was a Mr Albert Ellis, a stationer and newsagent. He explained that he had known the fugitive for eighteen months – 'as an author he had bought largely of foolscap and writing paper' – and, until recently, he had always looked upon him as 'a highly respectable sort of man'.

What had shaken Ellis' view was that, on the morning of the crime, Lefroy had asked him to call at Cathcart Road, claiming that Mrs Clayton wished to see some samples of stationery. The lady had, however, appeared surprised by Ellis' visit, and when he returned to his shop he found that Lefroy had visited it in his absence and swindled the boy who had been left in charge there.

As the latter described the incident, 'Mr Lefroy said he had come to pay a bill that was owing to Mr Ellis. He had an envelope fastened up and said it contained two sovereigns, and as this was over the amount due he would be obliged if I would give him the nineteen shillings change.'

Only when Ellis opened the envelope did he find that the 'sovereigns' were Hanoverian tokens similar, it appeared, to those that had since been found in the railway carriage and on Lefroy's person when searched by the police at Brighton.

Nor was the stationer's the only evidence of the fugitive's unorthodox methods of 'raising the wind'. The pawn tickets found in the coat he had abandoned at the Claytons were found to refer to articles pledged, under assumed names, in no fewer than four different pawnbrokers in districts extending from Croydon to the West End.

But it was left to the informative contributor to the *Daily Telegraph*, on this occasion referring to his subject's alleged love of cricket, to provide a near farcical note on Lefroy's impecunious adventuring. 'On a recent occasion', he related, 'Lefroy got up an eleven for a cricket match, his contingent being understood to be colonial journalists while, on the other side, were several well-known theatrical gentlemen. Lefroy's eleven lost, and when the wickets were drawn and he was required to pay his quota towards the expenses, he excused himself on the grounds that his bag had been opened and his purse extracted. It was subsequently found that other bags had been cut in a similar way ...'

Indeed, it would appear that although cricket seemed to be his principal diversion, his love of talking about his alleged achievements in the literary and theatrical fields ran the game a close second, as did his zest for prompting dubious 'deals'. He was an almost compulsive talker, and a plausible talker too, though to be fair he never appeared to be the richer for it.

As an example of the fugitive's considerable powers of persuasion, the *Telegraph* correspondent recalled with a touch of bitterness that some time ago he had shown Lefroy the manuscript of a small work he had composed and the latter, having read it, had then coolly proceeded to negotiate for the purchase of the document, until the contract, save for the actual legal formalities, was all but complete. Fortunately the manuscript was recovered ...

However, by the time such revealing anecdotes had appeared in print, Percy Lefroy Mapleton – 'stage title' Arthur Lefroy – was playing the star part in a tragedy that, more garish than even the most lurid of his rejected plots, was to succeed where the latter had so singularly failed – namely in big billing for his name.

A police watch on all trains for the continent, a watch on shipping leaving the Channel ports, and publicity surrounding both murder and murderer unsurpassed since the time of the Muller case – by the end of the week the authorities were using every means at their disposal to trace Lefroy and bring him to justice.

The *Daily Telegraph* had obtained and published a picture of the wanted man and made newspaper history in the process. The Yard had added a pen and ink portrait to its previous description and had also printed the facsimile of a letter Lefroy had recently sent to a business acquaintance, just in case someone might recognise the handwriting. A description of his 'wounds' had been obtained from the Royal County Hospital, and staffs of casualty wards were alerted in case he should go to them for further treatment.

Finally it was announced that 'the Secretary of State for the Home Office will advise the grant of Her Majesty's gracious pardon to any accomplice, not being the person who actually committed the Murder, who shall give such evidence as shall lead to a like result'.

Yet still Lefroy remained at large.

There was, of course, no lack of rumour regarding the course of the hunt, or the alleged movements of the hunted. On Wednesday morning a coastguard had visited the Brighton police to report that a man answering to Lefroy's description had been seen in the town just after dawn, looking pale and wretched, as though he had spent the night tramping the streets. By Wednesday night the current yarn was that Lefroy had been arrested in Highgate, a story so widely believed that the Yard were forced to issue a denial, just in time to stop the story appearing in the morning papers. Only later did the authorities feel free to reveal that, with his head still bandaged, Lefroy had been seen that same day at the Fever Hospital, Islington.

Yet while the Press and the public, impatient for results, were daily becoming more censorious of the police handling of the search, the man in charge of its overall direction maintained his customary air of robust confidence. As head of the Detective Department at Scotland Yard, Chief Superintendent Williams was convinced that, despite reports of 'sightings' from people as far apart as Margate and Aberdeen, the fugitive had gone to earth in London and that, to use another hunting metaphor, shortage of resources would soon force him to break cover.

Given the sense of public outrage aroused by the nature of the crime the widespread sympathy for its victim, and the inducement to informers afforded by the reward, Lefroy's freedom, Williams reasoned, would not last for long.

In fact the Chief Superintendent, as he reviewed the situation on the Saturday, displayed an equanimity that embraced not only the apprehension of the suspect, but also the progress of that suspect's subsequent trial. For, while public attention had understandably been focused on the search for Lefroy, fresh evidence had come to hand that, should the search succeed, would help to ensure his conviction.

On the day after the crime the LBSCR had mobilised a strong force of labourers to search the track between Croydon and Preston no fewer than a dozen men being assigned to the narrow stretch between the Balcombe Tunnel and the Ouse Viaduct, to the south of Balcombe Station.

Although the search failed to uncover the revolver that had fired the rounds in the murder coach, it had yielded two other clues: a blood-stained shirt collar, subsequently identified as Lefroy's and the hat that had been worn by Mr Gold.

This last discovery was of particular interest to Williams. The hat had been found ten miles south of the spot where Gold's body had been discovered, so that to have thrown it out of the carriage at that point his murderer must still have been on the train.

Also a woman had come forward, a Mrs Brown, who could claim to be almost an eye-witness – although at very long range – of the start of the killer's ferocious attack. On Monday afternoon, Mrs Brown and her young daughter had been looking out of the window of their cottage, King's Head Cottage, Horley, when the 2.10 roared by. And, just for a split second, they had caught a glimpse of two men standing up in a first-class carriage, men who appeared to be fighting.

At the time they had not pursued the matter – 'it could have been the men were only larking' – and it was not until they heard of the murder hunt that they thought fit to inform the police of what they had seen.

To the Yard this new evidence had come as a substantial bonus, the more welcome because it was totally unexpected. As Horley was some eight miles down the line from Merstham Tunnel – where those 'loud explosions' had so frightened Gibson's boy – it confirmed that the assailant had struck at a comparatively early stage of the journey, and the resultant struggle had been hard-fought and protracted, a fact that, taken in conjunction with yet another development – the testimony of Gold's widow at the coroner's inquest – helped to clarify another source of doubt.

Strongly built and in robust health, Gold should have proved more than a match, despite his age, for the weedy, consumptive-looking Lefroy, a fact that had not only puzzled Williams, but had also served to give some credence to the suspect's initial story of a burly and rough-looking fellow traveller, seated opposite to Mr Gold.

Another puzzle was that the doctor who had first examined Gold's body had said he could find no trace of a bullet wound, even though Dr Hall, at the Sussex County Hospital, had referred to the marks on the dead man's face as possibly having been caused by the muzzle blast of a revolver, fired at close range. And to confuse things still further, there was Hall's original testimony that the marks on Lefroy's scalp could have been caused by pressure from the barrel of a small pistol. He had also a graze behind the ear that could have been caused by a bullet.

Was it possible that the victim – not the murderer – had carried the gun, if gun there was? Had Gold fired the shots in self-defence and narrowly missed? The theory was a plausible one, but speedily demolished by the widow who said that the only firearm possessed by the Gold household was an old-fashioned blunderbuss which had been in store for nearly forty years. 'My husband was too nervous a man to carry arms,' she said. 'He was of a very timid disposition. At the least thing he got nervous.'

Indeed, she had dwelt at some length upon this theme and, in doing so, had involuntarily supplied her audience with a fascinating, if somewhat daunting, insight into the character of the man for whom she now wore black.

Gold, though retired, had by no means been inactive in the pursuit of profit. He had owned a corn chandler's shop in Walworth, one of several shrewd investments, and had been collecting the takings on the day he was murdered. It would appear that he was also something of a miser, and afflicted by the worries inseparable from that role.

'He had a great fear of anyone getting into his bedroom at night,' said Mrs Gold. 'He always locked the bedroom door.' Except when on his way to the bank with the weekly takings, he never carried more than a handful of silver. He did not like to have much money about his person, she explained. He had been 'close' in money matters, even with her.

But revealing though such anecdotes might be, the most interesting part of Mrs Gold's evidence related to her late husband's travel arrangements. He hated the journey to London because it brought him into contact with strangers, and his fear and suspicion of strangers was so great as to be almost obsessional. Usually, she said, he would shut his eyes and feign sleep to discourage fellow passengers from talking to him. He was convinced that people were prying into his affairs and was afraid of being tricked into giving them information. So he would shut his eyes and appear to be lost in slumber.

At last the picture was beginning to take shape. The sight of a prosperous elderly gentleman dozing peacefully in his corner seat might well discourage those whose only purpose was a harmless chat about politics or the weather, but conversely it could also serve to make him tempting prey to others with a more criminal intent.

Say that one such, revolver in hand, had thought to take the 'sleeper' by surprise? And say that, instead, it was he who had been surprised

– surprised by the sleeper's sudden awakening? What would have followed next? As Williams saw it, a violent struggle in which Gold, perhaps stunned or wounded by a first shot, had grabbed desperately at the gun arm of his assailant, causing the latter to miss. And then, after the bullets had plunged into the coachwork and seats, a further struggle had ensued in which the robust old man had continued to hold his own until the robber, grazed by the powder blast, reached for his knife.

But it was while he was still contemplating this likely sequence of events that the Superintendent's conviction of Lefroy's guilt received its greatest fillip – the discovery of the murdered man's umbrella. It had been found at the side of the track, fully twenty miles from the place where they had found the hat, and well south of Hassocks Station. And, as Hassocks had been the only point where the 2.10 had slowed sufficiently for a man to jump from the train with even the faintest chance of avoiding death or serious injury, this proved – and proved conclusively – that Mr Gold's attacker was still aboard the train when it arrived at Preston Park.

Moreover, the umbrella – like every other item belonging to the dead man – was soaked in blood. Yet only one of the passengers interviewed at Preston had blood-stains on his clothing, and that man was Lefroy. The case against the fugitive looked very black indeed, and equally black looked the chances of his evading its consequences.

The wide advertisement of his appearance and mannerisms, his comparative ignorance of the underworld that alone could give him refuge, and the fact that, with every 'respectable' haven completely barred to him, he would be at the mercy of that underworld's greediest villains – narks and informers hungry for reward. All these were factors that weighed heavily against the chances of Lefroy continuing at liberty much longer. If 'liberty' it could be called when, though inspired by vastly different motives, the hands of saints and sinners alike were turned against him.

It was a little after eleven on the morning of Thursday 30 June that a young man calling himself Clarke arrived outside the widow Bickers' house at 32 Smith Street, Stepney, studied the 'bedroom 'to let' sign that graced the grimy first-floor window, and then knocked at the door to inquire how much she would charge in rent.

When Mrs Bickers had shown him the room and told him that it would cost 6s a week, he said it would suit him perfectly. He would move in that same day. He was an engraver, just down from Liverpool, he explained, and his luggage would follow later.

Clarke, as the landlady was to recall in later years, seemed 'a nice young man, very pale and delicate-looking' and paid 3s 6d in advance towards his rent without the smallest quibble. He also appeared to be extremely undemanding, though on Saturday, when told the lodgers dined together on a Sunday, he excused himself from conforming to that tradition of the house on the grounds that he would be busy in his room. However, as if to make up for this lack of sociability, he had paid the landlady a further 2s 6d, thus settling the rent for the entire week.

It was on Saturday that Mrs Bickers asked him if she could borrow his newspaper, the *London Daily News*. 'There has been a murder on the Brighton line,' she said, 'and I would like to read all about it.'

Later, after reading of the police hunt for Lefroy, she again raised the subject of the murder, and asked her lodger, 'Have they caught that man yet – the man who murdered the rich old fellow on the train?' But he did not seem to share her interest in the subject, and merely answered, 'I do not think so'.

In a few days' time Mrs Bickers would herself be prominently featured in the daily newspapers. She would also have the mortification of seeing her Smith Street residence described therein as 'a dingy lodging house in the squalid East End'. But at the time of her brief chat with young Clarke she had no premonition of this notoriety to come, and entertained a certain pride in the character of her establishment. The previous tenant of the new lodger's room had occupied it for over three years, she proudly told him, 'and I hope that you will stay for just as long.' It was hope that, alas, was soon to wither.

For one who was so professedly 'busy', the engraver did not appear to get out and about very much. Even on Tuesday morning when he announced his intention of leaving the house at 5am the following day, this early departure turned out to be for the purpose of visiting the public bath-house before the crowds arrived. All through Wednesday he stayed closeted in his room, seemingly shunning the sunshine.

It was on Thursday that a letter arrived for him, a letter that he had been anxious about almost since the day of his arrival. Mistakenly he had given his address as No. 33 and he had told the landlady that he was worried lest in consequence his correspondence might go astray. But when she went up to his room to hand him the letter she found the door locked and had to slide the letter under it. It was not until noon that Clarke referred to the matter, and then only indirectly.

Coming downstairs with a piece of paper in his hand, he asked Mrs Bickers if she could take a cab and 'collect some money for me', but the landlady at that time had other things to do. 'Why can't you go yourself?' she asked him, not unreasonably, and was by no means convinced by his subsequent explanation that he had twisted his ankle when getting out of bed.

However, when Clarke than asked if she could get 'some respectable person' to send a telegram for him she recommended him to try a neighbour – a Mr Doyle – to whom he gave 1s 6d. '1s for the post office charge,' he said, 'and 6d for your trouble.'

Taking the telegram, Doyle noticed that it was addressed to a Mr Seale, at a firm in the City, and opened, sensibly enough, with a request to 'please bring my wages this evening about seven'. But the rest of the message – 'B' shall have the flour tomorrow' – seemed so unlikely that he assumed that it was some sort of secret code.

Otherwise, however, he did not give the matter much thought. After all, he was not to know that the home address of Mr Seale was 4 Cathcart Road in semi-rural Wallington. Nor that, for the past few months, Seale had been the room-mate and boon companion of that much wanted murderous villain known as Arthur Lefroy. Nor was the obliging Doyle to realise – until too late – that he had let £200 slip through his fingers. Instead, it was left to others to appreciate, and act upon, the vital clue provided by the telegram. And act on it they did ...

The police team that arrived in Smith Street, Stepney, on the evening of Friday 8 July was small in numbers, but formidable in rank. It consisted of only two men, Donald Swanson and Frederick Jarvis, but each was a full inspector in the CID with a long line of successes to his credit. For all the Yard knew, the fugitive whose refuge had now been traced to Mrs Bickers' lodging house at No. 32 might well have armed himself and be ready to offer violence. If he did, Swanson and Jarvis would be just the men to cope. Certainly they wasted no time in their assault.

Leaving Jarvis to keep guard outside the building, Swanson dashed straight up the stairs to the first-floor landing and hurled open the bedroom door. As he did so he ducked adroitly to one side flattening himself against the adjoining wall – a precaution, born of experience, against his quarry opening fire. But no shot came.

'Arthur Lefroy Mapleton?' It was not so much a question that Swanson shouted as a challenge and statement of fact.

'Yes, I was expecting you.' The voice was resigned, expressive almost of relief.

Although it was still daylight in the dusty street outside, the blinds and curtains had been drawn and the room was in semi-darkness. But as the Inspector peered warily around the door, he could just detect amid the shadows, the figure of a man, standing perfectly still, hands empty of any weapon.

'I am arresting you on the charge of murdering Mr Frederick Gold', said Swanson.

Pale-faced and unshaven, the man advanced into the light, quietly allowed the handcuffs to be placed around his wrists and then, on being cautioned, said: 'I am not obliged to make any reply, and I don't think I shall do so.'

Inspector Jarvis entered the room, repeated the charge and received the same answer with the added comment: 'Well, I will qualify that by saying I am not guilty.'

These formalities duly completed, the officers started to search the room and its few items of furniture, which included a rather battered chest of drawers. One of the drawers was locked, and when Lefroy was asked for the key he answered that he had not been given one. He said, somewhat excitedly, that the drawer 'was impossible to move', and when Jarvis proved the falsity of this by forcing it open, it was found to contain a black cloth waistcoat and a black scarf stained with blood. In other drawers were two cloth caps, a pair of false whiskers to hook over the ears, a false moustache and a pair of scissors.

Later, when Jarvis was making an inventory of the prisoner's effects, Lefroy was asked if the scissors were his or if they belonged to the house.

'They are mine,' he answered, adding unconcernedly, 'I used them to cut off my moustache and whiskers.'

When 'Mr Clarke' accompanied by his escorts left No. 32 in a closed cab, he still contrived to preserve his calm and almost affable manner, even confiding in an aside to Swanson, 'I am glad you found me for I was sick and tired of it all. I should have given myself up in a day or two, but I could not bear the exposure; I feared certain matters in connection with my family would be made public.' He bitterly regretted the fact that he had run away because, he said, 'it puts such a different complexion on the case.' At the police station, the prisoner returned to his theme of repentance, and repeatedly stated how relieved he had been to find that the officers had tracked him down. 'I was really wretched, I had nothing to eat all day', he told them.

But he subsequently asked if he could see a lawyer, and when Jarvis answered 'Certainly' he commented sombrely, 'I am glad you did not bring any of my so-called friends from Wallington with you.' Professedly glad though he might be at his arrest, it was plain that he felt that Mr Seale had little claim upon his gratitude.

A rum character, this so-called Arthur Lefroy, author, journalist and actor. The more Jarvis saw of him the more puzzled he was, and in the next forty-eight hours it was Jarvis's fortune to see him quite a lot.

Chosen, together with Swanson, to escort the prisoner by rail to Lewes Jail the day after the arrest, he found him to be not only calm but positively nonchalant, chatting and smoking as if the journey was a pleasurable excursion instead of the one that was carrying him to the grim, grey prison on the top of the Sussex Downs, and possibly to the hangman's rope as well.

Only once was there any break in his apparent composure, and this the officers felt to be of profound significance. As the train began its approach to the Balcombe Tunnel, Lefroy showed by the quick movements of his gestures and glances signs of increasing nervous agitation, and, as it passed through the tunnel itself, he became so excitable that he was unable to speak. However, the two inspectors had little time to dwell on this phenomenon, for the next step was Haywards Heath where escort and prisoner had to change trains, and by then they were somewhat excitable too.

Although still primarily devoted to agriculture, that pleasant market town had already become – thanks to the facilities afforded by the LBSCR – a popular dormitory area for well-to-do business folk obliged to pursue their daily livelihood in London. And among such regular patrons of train travel the Gold murder had aroused a personal fear and resentment.

Scarcely had Jarvis and Swanson got their man on to the platform than they were greeted with hoots and jeers from a group of passengers tipped off as to his identity. The news spreading, others joined in the tumult and they were hard put to it to reach the Lewes train which they bundled him aboard with the help of the station staff.

A porter having locked the door of the carriage against intruders, they pulled down the blinds across its windows, not only to hide Lefroy from the public gaze, but also as a protection against flying glass should the crowd turn to stone-throwing. But law-abiding Haywards Heath had its good reputation to preserve and prisoner and escort alike emerged unscathed from this lively confrontation with its residents who were

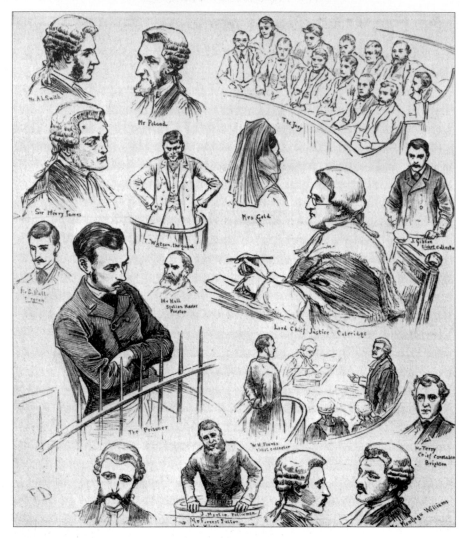

Artist's impression of the Lefroy trial as viewed from the press gallery.

Montagu Stephen Williams.

content with purely oral protests, which continued at high pitch until the train pulled out.

Throughout this brief but rather frightening incident, Lefroy, though turning even paler than usual, had shown no sign of panic. Even on his arrival at Lewes, where a prison van was waiting for him in the station forecourt, he continued to impress his guardians with his – doubtless contrived – appearance of sang-froid. In fact, they had a suspicion that he was almost enjoying being the cynosure of so much hostile attention, the actor in him responding to the strength and colour of his role.

He must indeed be a regular 'rare-un', Jarvis reflected, to take it all so calmly, particularly when the odds were so against him. Indeed the odds were even more against him now, for while the prisoner had still been at large in Stepney fresh evidence had come to hand concerning the nature of the injuries sustained by Mr Gold and the identity of the weapon that had inflicted them.

On 2 July, Thomas Bond MRCS, a prominent lecturer in forensic medicine, had been called to the Yard to consider the separate testimonies of Dr Hall and Dr Byass, which differed widely over the question of whether the dead man had been shot. After a thorough examination of the body he had revealed that Dr Hall had been correct in his diagnosis. A wound near the eye extended to the vertebrae of Gold's neck, in the second of which the specialist found a 'bullet the size of a pea'. This fact at last established, the search for the murder weapon itself, although intensified, had still proved fruitless, but a vital clue had been obtained regarding the revolver's ownership. A man matching the description of Lefroy, but giving the name of Lee, had pledged a small-calibre revolver at Messrs Adams & Helstead, pawnbrokers in the Borough, on 21 June. He had redeemed the pledge on the morning of the 29th, a few hours before the murder, and, while the pawn tickets found in the prisoner's blood-stained clothing at Cathcart Road were for other items, pledged in other shops, the names 'Lee' and also 'Leigh' were written on them. The evidence for the prosecution seemed complete.

Lefroy was brought to trial before Lord Chief Justice Coleridge at the Maidstone Assizes on Friday 4 November 1881. Leading for the prosecution was the Attorney General, Sir Henry James, later Lord James of Hertford. The prisoner had the services of Mr Montagu Williams, regarded as an extremely able barrister, noted for the unorthodoxy and daring of his tactics, and the powerful appeals he was wont to make to the emotions of a jury.

Though far removed from the metropolis, and therefore far less vulnerable to the mob excesses that had accompanied Muller's trial and

Lord Chief Justice Coleridge.

subsequent execution, the Maidstone court, to quote a contemporary, was 'crowded in every part' when the proceedings opened, and the police found difficulty in clearing its approaches.

The case had aroused such extensive interest that the audience inside the courtroom was by no means confined to the curious and the vulgar. Prominent local notables were also present, including the High Sheriff of Kent, while among the hundreds left in the street outside were many who had travelled down from London on a special excursion ticket.

Yet by the second day of the trial much of this enthusiasm had waned, and a correspondent of the county newspaper reported with evident surprise: 'The space for spectators was thrown open at half-past nine, and it was gradually occupied, but there was no crowding.' The pavement outside the court 'was almost deserted'.

What was the reason for this sudden fall in the trial's, mass appeal? Certainly it did not stem from the conduct of its principals.

The accused himself had done his best to give full value to his audience, even requesting that he be allowed to redeem his frockcoat from pawn in order to present a more impressive appearance. This being refused, he had prevailed upon his warders to allow him to carry his topper, the newest item of his slender wardrobe and evidently a source of considerable personal pride. Indeed, there were times when he appeared to be more intent on admiring its glossy brim and adding a fresh sheen to it than listening to the exchanges taking place in the court around him.

Nor had Sir Henry, in opening the case for the prosecution or Williams, with his barbed cross-examination of the prosecution witnesses, by any means underplayed their roles for the occasion. Each of these protagonists was at the top of his form.

But the cooling of public interest in this well-billed, well-cast production, was a fatal deficiency in the plot. After the excitements of Friday's first act, ranging from 'The Finding of the Corpse' to 'The Arrest of the Suspect', what else was there left to enjoy, or marvel at? The best was over.

Again, until the opening of the drama, there was doubt – widespread doubt – about the nature of its ending. But by Saturday morning that doubt had almost vanished. After Sir James' lucid summary, lasting one hour and four minutes, of the events leading up to Lefroy's committal, and the evidence offered by the long string of witnesses produced by the prosecution, even the keenest believer in the innocence of the man in the dock must have felt the need to make a considerable reassessment.

Of course there had been discrepancies here and there in such a rich flow of evidence, and Montagu Williams had been quick to latch on to them.

Inspector Howland of the railway company's police had testified that, when searched at Brighton, Lefroy had said of the watch: 'That is mine – that is my watch.' But, after a fierce cross-examination, Howland was forced to confess that: 'I made no entry in my book that the prisoner said that.'

There had been some confusion among the railwaymen at Preston Park about which of them had been the first to spot the watch and chain protruding from the prisoner's boot. The ticket collector, Gibson? His colleague? The guard of the 2.10? Or the station-master, Mr Hall? Skilfully, Williams had hit at the credibility of all four by implying that each of them was jealously trying to hog the glory.

William Franks, ticket collector at London Bridge, also came under the defence's fire. Franks' evidence had been to the effect that he had stood on the platform beside the carriage occupied by Gold and Lefroy until the train pulled out, and therefore could testify that no mysterious 'third person' had then joined them. But this was part-countered by Williams' use of the chemist Gibson. Cross-examined, the latter said: 'I do not remember seeing Mr Franks positioned on the platform'.

Yet despite counsel's brave attempt to make the most of such slips, they were of minor importance when compared to the cumulative weight of the evidence against the prisoner.

Whatever Lefroy had said – or not said – during his interrogation by Howland, the fact remained that he had at no time intimated, either to Howland or anyone else, that the watch was not his own.

Similarly, all four of the station staff at Preston Park were at least unanimous in confirming that the watch and chain were in Lefroy's boot at the time they saw him, however much they might disagree about which of them had been the first to notice it.

And as for Franks, his presence on the platform could surely have passed unheeded by a passenger who, busy with his small son, was not likely to have kept his gaze fixed permanently on the carriage window.

In any case, Lefroy's own statements were so full of contradictions that such lapses on the part of the prosecution witnesses seemed comparatively trivial.

First alleging that he could remember nothing except a loud explosion, then claiming that two fellow passengers had been present in the carriage, one of whom had attacked him with a gouge (later amended to 'revolver'), and then providing (for a third source) a graphic description of how both men had attacked him before 'getting out on to the road' and leaving him with several bullets in his head – the conflict between Lefroy's various statements about the so-called 'assault' had been neatly summarised by James in his address for the prosecution. Nor had the prisoner's reported comments on the 'flash sovereigns' found on the floor of the coach done anything to enhance his reputation for veracity.

At Preston Park he had said he knew nothing about them. At Brighton he had repeated this assertion. Yet after the police, overcoming his vigorous protests, had searched his clothing and extracted two similar coins, he had answered, 'I suppose I must have got them playing at whist!'

But probably the factor that had inflicted the most damage on the defence, during the first day of the trial, was the attitude of Judge Coleridge, whose interventions were so frequent as to seem almost excessive, and on Saturday they continued to be so, with nine-tenths of them heavily loaded against the prisoner.

When, in the late afternoon, Williams rose to deliver the concluding speech for the defence, even he must have inwardly conceded that the battle was lost. Indeed, whatever the skill of his delivery and however eloquent his address, his plea could be said to have been lost before it had even begun. However, whatever the nature of his own thoughts. Montagu Williams kept them to himself.

Doomed or not, it was a brave defence. It was also an extremely risky one. But Williams, in daring to essay it, showed that he had lost none of his nerve and cunning. Faced by the prosecution's detailed exposure of the glaring and repeated inconsistencies in his client's narrative, he argued that at the time Lefroy was still confused by the effects of the 'assault'. As for his subsequent flight, it was the nervous reaction of an imaginative young man alarmed by the continuous questioning to which he had been subjected. A romancer was not necessarily a murderer.

But it was when he witheringly described the whole case for the prosecution as resting on evidence that was largely circumstantial that Williams was at his most audacious. Pouring scorn on the prosecution's emphasis that it had been the habit of Mr Gold 'that very precise man' – to travel to London each Monday to collect his money, and also his habit on the last Monday of each month to bring home part of that money for housekeeping purposes, he scathingly asked, 'Is there a tittle of evidence to show that the prisoner knew anything of Mr Gold, let alone his habits? Is there an atom of evidence to show that the prisoner had seen Mr Gold before in the whole of his natural life?' Of course there was not.

'Is it probable,' he asked, 'that a man who meant to commit murder would prelude it by a fraud, and equip himself with visiting cards giving his true name and address? And why, if he had that morning redeemed a pistol from the pawnbrokers – redeemed it with the intention of employing it in his crime – should he have carried pawnbroking duplicates in his pockets?'

There was more – much more – to the same purpose, with Williams casting doubt on every hypothesis advanced by the prosecution.

Mrs Nye Chart, the Brighton theatre proprietress, had said that she knew nothing of his client. But Lefroy, who contributed to the Era, had said that he went down to see her. Was that so unlikely? The prosecution had alleged that Lefroy, because he looked into several carriages of the train before boarding the compartment occupied by Mr Gold, had been 'looking from carriage to carriage for his victim'. But there was not 'an atom of evidence to support that theory'.

And, on Lefroy's story of the escape of his 'assailant', Williams reminded the jury of the prosecution's claim that this was impossible to support because the lowest speed of the train had been thirty miles per hour. 'Yet, under close questioning, the guard of that train had revealed that at one stage, Hassocks Gate, it had slowed to a mere crawl.
Was it not possible then that the real murderer was the 'third' man in the carriage, as the prisoner had always claimed? And could not this 'third man', having stunned Lefroy and murdered the old gentleman, have indeed 'gone on to the way at Hassocks Gate?'

It was, as already noted, a brave defence. Several jurymen were reportedly in tears when Williams had come to the end of it. But tears that flow too readily are often as readily dried, and the Lord Chief Justice was quick to apply the comfort of a handkerchief.

Opening with a rather invidious reminder of 'the kind of persons with whom we have to deal', he said that, on the one hand there was the victim: 'An elderly man, a man of good means, retired from business, taking every week £30 or £40; regular in his habits, but a silent man, who rather shrank from conversation with others; a man of some physical strength, a large-made man in full health; but, at the same time, it is to be remembered that, at his age – sixty-four – a man's strength is not what it was."

There were certain things about the man, the judge continued, that were worth attention. He was a person who usually carried two purses, in one of them gold, in the other silver. He wore double eye-glasses and he carried a gold watch with a chain that went round his neck. He also carried pocket books, but he never carried firearms. Such was a sketch of the bodily and mental character of Mr Gold. The prisoner was a person very different in all respects.

And then, to ensure that the jury should have no possible doubt about what he meant by Lefroy being 'very different', His Lordship emphasised: 'He is without money, curiously erratic in his habits, not scrupulous in regard to honesty, and of his early life, how brought up, and in company with what associates, we know nothing.' Not, he hastened to add, that these 'unfavourable circumstances' had been mentioned to suggest that, because the prisoner would cheat, he would also murder, 'but merely to show the sort of man he was, and the temptations to which his life exposed him'.

Such was the start of a lengthy and eloquent summing-up that, while scrupulously fair in its presentation of the factual evidence, would seem, even by the standards then prevailing, to have been so weighted against the prisoner that it would have more properly been presented by the prosecution.

Indeed, when it came to his subsequent reconstruction of the setting of the crime itself, Coleridge could well have been accused of 'piling on the agony' for the benefit of the jury, and it was noticeable that Lefroy, abandoning his complacent study of his hat, sat stiff and rigid in the dock, staring wide-eyed at the judge as if for the first time appreciating the extent of his danger.

'At Merstham four shots were heard', the judge recalled. 'That was seventeen miles from London; and at twenty-five miles, at Horley, a struggle was seen going on in the carriage.' The struggle would take some time. Mr Gold was a powerful man, but there was a knife as well as a revolver, and he had fourteen knife wounds. The body was thrown out, probably with life still in it, at the entrance to the Balcombe Tunnel, thirty-one miles from London, so that the struggle lasted for eight miles.

And then slowly and impressively he continued: 'This is an awful thing to contemplate, and what terrible incidents it must have given rise to! It reminds one of the *Haunted House* by Hood, the story of a victim at once caged and hunted.

'The struggle must have been long and protracted. It began with the firing of a revolver, with the wounding of Mr Gold, and his assailant went on till he had succeeded in casting his victim out, still alive, still struggling, as was shown by that dreadful piece of evidence, the marks of blood-stained fingers on the footboard. '

Eloquent stuff, and picturesque. No jury could fail to be moved by so evocative a summary of the horrors of the crime, or miss its implication: the need for condign punishment. Nor was it difficult for the court to see that the criminal, although Coleridge was careful not to say as much, was in his opinion no other than the man who stood before him in the dock.

But if His Lordship, not usually the most severe of judges, could be accused of having strayed a little from the strict impartiality traditional to his role, it was perhaps because he saw – and saw so clearly – the fatal flaw in Williams' case for the defence.

The 2.10 had indeed slowed down at Hassocks Gate, slowed so that the 'third man' – had there been one – could well have jumped on to the track and escaped uninjured. But the murdered man's umbrella, as previously mentioned, had been found beyond this point. It had been lying to the south of it, much nearer to Brighton.

Mr Gold's killer had been aboard the train when it stopped at Preston Park, and, this accepted, the evidence· against Lefroy ceased to be 'purely circumstantial'. The links in the chain (reminiscent of the Muller case) were continuous and strong.

It took the jury only ten minutes to reach their verdict. Inevitably, it was 'Guilty'.

After the Judge had pronounced the death sentence, prefacing its awful details with the reflection that 'You have been justly and rightly convicted, and it is right and just that you should die', Lefroy, playing the part of wronged hero to the last, turned towards the jury box and said, 'Gentlemen of the jury, some day, when too late, you will learn that you have murdered me.'

Percy Lefroy Mapleton was hanged at Lewes Jail on 29 November, just twenty days after the conclusion of the trial. And he died after making one final gesture to the gallery by confessing that his previous pose, as persecuted innocent, had been false, though he had never intended to murder Mr Gold. He had not, it would appear, intended to murder anyone.

Almost bankrupt as a result of his efforts to mix with Society and be one of the theatrical and literary set, he had, in desperation, got his revolver out of pawn, travelled to London Bridge, and there, with what was left of the 'change' from his transaction with the stationer's boy, purchased the first-class single ticket to Brighton that was to have meant the mending of his fortunes.

He had boarded the train, he said, in the hope of 'holding-up' a likely passenger, maybe a defenceless lady who could be frightened into parting with her purse the painless way. He had killed Gold only when made desperate by the old gentleman's stout resistance.

The passing of Percy Lefroy was mercifully free of the horrific mob licence that had disgraced the public hanging of Franz Muller. The crowd that had waited outside the prison walls for the raising of the black flag, the only visual sign that sentence had been duly executed, was numbered in scores rather than in thousands and its attitude was more funereal than excited or depraved.

The early morning had been cold with a slight fog rising from the river meadows that lay at the base of Castle Hill, but as the great bell of the prison began to toll – it had never before been used for an execution –'the sun shone brilliantly from out of a cloudless blue sky'.

It was still shining when, to again quote from *The Sussex Express*, 'at exactly nine o'clock the trap was heard to fall ... and slowly, but quietly, the bystanders started to make their way home'.

It had been a remarkably decorous audience – as hanging audiences go – and the *Express*, paying tribute to its good behaviour, was doubtless speaking for the vast majority in the county when it stated: 'The curtain has fallen on the last scene of the Brighton railway tragedy, and with it comes to many minds a profound feeling of relief.'

But, this notwithstanding, the paper still found space to spare a thought for the facilities designed to expedite the principal actor's exit, comparing them felicitously with those previously in use.

'Since Martin Browne suffered about 12 years ago, the arrangements for such shocking occasions have been considerably improved', the *Express* recorded.

'Browne had to climb a flight of steps to the scaffold, but the shifting plank on which Lefroy was launched into eternity was on a level with the ground upon which he walked from the prison door. Beneath had been dug a pit, about twelve feet deep and bricked around, into which the body of the malefactor descended.'

The virtue of this particular 'improvement', the paper explained, lay in the fact that 'instead of the executioner having to leave his man with arms and feet strapped while he went below to draw the bolt, all that had to be done was to move a lever, such as those used in shifting the points on railway lines.'

The *Express* concluded with the pleasing reflection that 'a more expeditious, not to say merciful, plan it would perhaps be impossible to devise'.

If 'improvements' had made the scaffold an easier place on which to die, improvements of a vastly different sort were exercising the minds of those responsible for the safety of the customers of the railway companies.

Just as after the murder of Thomas Briggs the rail-travelling public's clamour for reassurance had led to such eccentricities as the Muller Light, and eventually to the crude prototypes of the modern communication cord, so had the fate of Mr Gold aroused widespread doubts about the efficiency of the new devices and a call for renewed efforts to perfect them.

Immediately after the Brighton line tragedy the LBSCR directors had issued a statement that although neither the engine driver nor the guard had 'received any intimation' that anything untoward was happening, and therefore had failed to apply the brakes and investigate the matter, the electric alarm apparatus 'in accordance with the regulations of the company' had been tested at Croydon by the guard and found to be in working order.

To the more nervous type of rail passenger, however, this brought small consolation. An 'apparatus' might well be in working order, but equally the victim of a sudden attack might well be overwhelmed before he could reach it. Again, even should he succeed in his endeavour much would then depend on the warning bell the cord activated being heard by the crew above the din created by the train.

It was eight years after Mr Gold had embarked on his fatal journey that the government, in an Act of Parliament more far-reaching than its hesitant predecessor of 1865, obliged the railways to introduce a whole range of safety precautions, from the interlocking of points and signals to automatic braking, and a new communication cord system whereby the passenger could personally bring the train to an automatic halt.

Unfortunately, however, even this revolutionary improvement was to prove of no help at all to pretty Elizabeth Camp who, in 1897, was to die a few weeks before what was to have been her wedding day.

6

Wreath for a Bride

For Elizabeth it had been a lovely day, or so she told her elder sister, Mrs Haynes, who, having come to see her off at Hounslow Station, helped her lift her precious packages on to the luggage rack of the empty second-class compartment of the 7.42 for Waterloo. 'A lovey day,' she repeated breathlessly, regardless of the February cold.

Elizabeth had been to Hammersmith in the morning to visit her younger sister and had arrived at Hounslow at 5pm in time for tea. And in both places, which explained her happy excitement, she had been busy shopping in preparation for her wedding.

A really lovely day, a day to remember, and now it looked like being a lovely evening too, with Edward to meet her in the booking hall at the terminus before taking her out to the music-hall, and then escorting her home.

It had been a bit of a rush getting to the station. Mrs Haynes and a gentleman friend of the family had taken her to a local hotel to buy the bride-to-be a celebratory drink, and, chatting merrily, not one of them had noticed the clock. Elizabeth had been breathless and in quite a tizzy as she fumbled with her little green purse to find her ticket. And even though her sister and a grinning railway porter had tried to assure her there was enough time to spare, she had hitched up her skirt around her ankles, and had run for the waiting train as though pursued.

Edward Berry, the handsome young fruiterer from the Walworth Road, was a bit of a worrier about his future bride. Had she missed the train he would have fidgeted, and stayed fidgeting through all the time

The exterior of Waterloo Station, *circa* 1900.

he would spend waiting anxiously for the next – 'imagining the worst', the girls agreed.

It was, of course, extremely stupid of Edward to get so upset. Elizabeth had learned to look after herself when, still in her teens, she had started work as a barmaid at the Good Intent in East Street, Walworth, and had acquired additional self-reliance as a nurse at Winchmore Hill, before returning to the pub to serve as manageress.

Again, the train journey was so short and passed through such highly respectable suburbs, that not even the most timid of gently nurtured maidens had reason to fear an assault upon their virtue. The 7.42 would surely be picking up passengers at every one of the eight stops that lay between Hounslow and the terminus, headquarters of the London & South Western Railway. The journey itself would last for little more than forty minutes, arrival time at Waterloo being 8.23.

All the same, Edward's concern was more than a little flattering to one accustomed, in the 'trade', to ruder usage. 'You'd think I was a child,' Elizabeth used to say, 'instead of a woman of thirty, and weighing near thirteen stone – but as he feels that way, I like to keep him happy.'

The last her sister saw of the bride-to-be was a laughing face beneath a bobbing flowered hat and a gloved hand waving from the open carriage window. It was the last, apparently, that anyone was ever to see of Elizabeth – with the exception of her murderer – until her body was identified, approximately two hours later.

It was past 8.23. It was even past 8.30. And still there was no sign of Elizabeth. Waiting, as arranged, in the booking-hall at Waterloo, the eager Mr Berry, no end of a swell in his Derby hat and tight-fitting tweeds, looked hopefully for a glimpse of his sweetheart among the hurrying crowds, and looked in vain.

It was so unlike Lizzie to have tarried, knowing how anxious he became, and how he hated her travelling after dark, that at first he tried to persuade himself that the train was late, and got quite annoyed at the thought of it. The railways, so punctual in their main-line services, never seemed to care about the local 'stoppers'. It was too bad. He had tickets for the music-hall in his pocket. It would be a pity to waste them. But when the hands of the great clock above the hall crept round to 8.35, he discovered that, wherever the blame might lay, it certainly wasn't with the LSWR. 'The train arrived dead on time,' a porter protested. 'Came in twelve minutes ago!'

'Fidgeting' as foreseen, Berry briefly wondered if perhaps there had been a little misunderstanding. They had been more than a little excited when they had fixed the time and place of their rendezvous, so it would not be all that surprising. Perhaps she had thought he would meet her at the platform barrier, in which case she would be waiting for him on the platform itself.

At the thought of this, he went hurrying from the hall to the platform scheduled for the Hounslow service, only to find that, although the train was in, there was no trace of either Elizabeth or any other of the passengers. They had long since passed the barrier, the collector said.

It was just as he was about to inquire the time of the next arrival that he suddenly noticed that a small group of station officials were gathering along the platform around an open carriage door. They were making agitated gestures, and seemed in some sort of distress. Then, even as he watched, wondering what this signified, two men came pounding past him at the double, pushed the collector aside without a word of apology, and ran down the platform in haste to join the others. Both of them wore the uniform of the railway company's police.

An awful premonition swept over Edward Berry. A premonition of utter disaster. This sudden bustle, with its strong hint of panic – it was somehow concerned with Elizabeth, and he knew it. He tried to thrust the dreadful thought aside, but failed.

Pointing tremblingly at the policeman, who by then had reached the group around the open door, he said to the ticket collector: 'It looks as though they'fe lifted something out of the train and have lowered it on the platform.' But the other made no reply.

Berry took another look, just in time to see the men unexpectedly bow their heads, and, as if on command, remove their caps. 'Has there,' he faltered, 'been some sort of accident?'

It was a carriage cleaner, sweeping litter from the train, who had found Elizabeth. Her body had been bundled face upwards beneath the carriage seat, and he almost tripped over her legs, spread apart across the carriage floor. Around them was a pool of blood that, glittering beneath the station lights, seemed almost to move towards him. Terrified, he had yelled at some passing porters to come to his assistance and they, in turn, had sent for the police.

A horrific sight met the men's eyes as they lifted the body out on to the platform. As they saw what the killer had done to the face of his victim, two of them burst into tears. Elizabeth had been battered to death, after staging what must have been an extremely fierce resistance. Her skull had been smashed in by blows from a blunt instrument, and the flesh around her torn lips and broken cheekbones, was black with bruises. Her umbrella, broken in two, was heavily blood-stained, and there was blood upon the cushions and the wall.

It was only after the corpse had been placed upon a stretcher and its gruesome wounds concealed by a tarpaulin, that Edward Berry was able to obtain even the briefest outline of the tragedy. The name of the victim was, at that stage, unknown to those who had found her, and it was only after both the stretcher and its burden had been removed in a horse ambulance, and he had followed it to St Thomas' Hospital, that he learned for sure that his terrifying premonition had come true.

And it was not until he was called upon to assist in the work of identification that, heart-broken and sick, he began to realise the full horror of what had happened, and the extent of the savagery that had been employed to destroy the pretty young woman who was to have been his bride.

Was Elizabeth's death the result of a chance encounter? Was robbery the motive inspiring her ruthless killer, or was there perhaps something else? Descending on Waterloo at the first hint of the tragedy and equally prompt in anticipating the questions their readers would be asking once the news appeared in print, the pressmen did not find the company's police anxious to hazard an answer. Searching the carriage they had found one significant clue, or at least they had thought it significant at the time – a pair of bone cuff-links near where the body had lain.

Significant also was the fact that they could find no trace of the dead woman's railway ticket. As this had not been included in the contents of her pocket, it was presumed that she had carried it in a purse that the killer had taken. Yet the robbery motive proved, on second thoughts, less easy to sustain.

The victims of the two previous train murders had been persons of substance and had looked the part. With their gold watch-chains, their discreet but expensive clothing, and the fact that they had chosen to travel 'first', each must have seemed a tempting target, a fat pigeon worth the plucking. But Elizabeth, too, had looked just what she was: a healthy young woman of the working classes.

True, her silver ear-rings were of some modest value, but, curiously, the 'thief' had left them alone. Her umbrella had been broken, but still retained its silver head. Her brooch had been left in place, as had her ring. Though confident, as the directors of the company rather prematurely declared, of 'apprehending the criminal', the police confessed to being undecided as to the motive for the crime.

The following day Superintendent Robinson, speaking at a hastily convened equivalent of what today would be called a press conference, gave a vivid account of the conjectured course of the struggle inside the carriage.

'The deceased apparently sat with her back to the engine. Her assailant probably first hit her a blow on the forehead, partially stunning her. She must have then grappled with the man, for splashes of blood were found on the opposite side of the carriage, and her umbrella was found broken. It is supposed that the murderer then swung round and inflicted a second blow on the left side of the head, smashing the skull and killing her.' But the motive, he admitted, still remained obscure.

'With the exception of a green purse, a small sum of money, and a second-class ticket from Hounslow, nothing was missing from the person of Miss Camp,' he replied to further questioning.

Elizabeth's killer, it would appear, had worked for meagre returns. Yet if the 'robbery' motive looked somewhat less sound than before, what else could have occasioned so odious a crime?

It had been suggested that the murdered girl might perhaps have encountered a sex fiend, a would-be rapist, a man who had disposed of her through panic lest her screams led to his capture.

Disappointingly, for stories of rape made compelling reading to Victorian ladies, this theory, too, had its shortcomings. A preliminary medical examination had confirmed that Elizabeth had not been sexually assaulted, and though this immunity could, of course, owe much to the strength of her resistance, in some respects a sex motive appeared unlikely.

Why, for instance, should the 'fiend' have selected for his foul deed a train that, though relatively sparse in passengers, was billed to stop at no fewer than eight stations, each of them, on average, only five minutes apart? And why should he have taken the risk of picking on Elizabeth, for all her prettiness a strongly built young woman, and capable of staging a fierce resistance, when he could have selected an easier prey? There was much about the 'sex fiend' formula that made little sense.

However, for Chief Detective Inspector Marshall the major urgency was not so much the unravelling of the motive as the need to lay hands upon the murderer, an objective he pursued with considerable enthusiasm.

In charge of the CID team that had been sent by Scotland Yard to reinforce the railway police – then only poorly equipped to cope with such rarities as murder – Marshall had been quick to spot the fact that the blood of the victim was still warm when she had been taken to St Thomas's. This signified that death occurred towards the end of the journey, from which he inferred that the killer, if not continuing to the terminus, must have quit the train at one of the last three stops: Putney, Wandsworth or Vauxhall. But after closely questioning the staffs of the stations concerned, Marshall, like Robinson, had reluctantly to concede that, so far, his investigations had drawn a blank.

In contrast to the crowds who crammed the peak period trains on the suburban line, the passenger load carried by the 7.42 on its Waterloo run was usually light. The train was timed just a shade too late to engage the custom of those who, sallying from the leafy groves of Isleworth and Kew, sought the joys afforded by 'a night up West'. And it was timed just a shade too early for urban excursionists to use it for their return trip to London. In fact it was only its westward trip, with late-night passengers from the City, that made the service financially worthwhile.

As a result Marshall had not unnaturally supposed that any suspicious behaviour or peculiarity of appearance on the part of a passenger seeking to leave the train at an intermediate stop along the line would have been observed by station staff, comparatively idle as they were at that time in the evening.

To judge by Elizabeth Camp's loss of blood, the criminal must have carried on his clothing some traces at least of the nature of his crime, but not one of the men interviewed appeared to have noticed anything unusual. The lamplight at the stations was strong enough for an inspector to read the small type on a ticket, yet blood-stains had passed unnoticed.

In fact, the Inspector's theory regarding the time and district in which the murderer struck was beginning to look fairly thin when a renewed and painstaking search of the track unexpectedly confirmed it.

A pestle. A chemist's pestle. It was made of porcelain with a wooden handle, and was twelve inches long. Its head measured slightly over eight inches in circumference. Stamped on the porcelain, at its juncture with the handle, was the figure 9.

But what distinguished this pestle from all others of its kind were the strands of hair – human hair – attached to it, secured firmly by a patch of congealed blood. That, and the fact that it had been found on the embankment at Mount Pleasant, almost midway between Wandsworth and Putney, and less than eight miles from Waterloo, showed Marshall's hunch had been justified.

Surely one of the most unusual murder weapons ever to fall into the hands of the Metropolitan Police, the pestle was a find of first-rate importance, and even before it had been confirmed that the hair upon it was that of the murdered woman, a major effort was launched to trace its origin and ownership.

The pestle was sent to Scotland Yard, where the unusual course was adopted of putting it on show to members of the public, in the hope that it might be recognised.

Inspired by a similar aim and encouraged by recollections of Fleet Street's contribution to the arrests of Muller and Lefroy, Marshall arranged for photographs of the pestle to be distributed to the Press, together with a description of certain special features that had been brought to light by the Yard's laboratory staff. 'It has a number of brass metal streaks, which suggest it has been used at brasswork, probably for pounding in a brass metal mortar.'

Conducted in an age when finger-printing was still unborn, and the science of forensic medicine not yet refined, the examination of the star exhibit had been as thorough as existing knowledge and resources would permit. Similar thoroughness characterised the search for human witnesses.

An appeal was made for all who had travelled on the 7.42 to report to their local police stations, and this initiative was rewarded the very next day by a passenger who came forward to reveal that he had seen a man get out of the train at Wandsworth on the night of the murder.

The man appeared to have been travelling in one of the rear coaches, and therefore would have been in the vicinity of the compartment that had been occupied by the unfortunate Miss Camp. 'He would have been about thirty years old,' the witness stated, 'with a dark moustache, and wearing a frockcoat and top hat.'

While the police issued an immediate appeal to this unknown traveller to make himself known so that he could 'assist in their inquiries', his alleged description was published in the Press and at every station in the LSWR network.

All were doomed to disappointment: the only person to answer the police call was a character who introduced himself to the startled station officer at Wandsworth as 'the man you're looking for – the murderer of Miss Camp'. Scotland Yard's quest was over, he asserted. He had murdered the young woman and was now ready to take the consequences.

Unfortunately, this obligingly frank informant turned out to be a mental case, a harmless freak who had not been within miles of the murder scene.

Nor were the police any luckier when they investigated a rumour circulating in the Vauxhall area. This was to the effect that a man with blood on his hands had been seen leaving the 7.42 at Vauxhall Station, and had later gone into a public house, calling agitatedly for spirits. The landlord had then noticed that there were blood-stains on his jacket, and had commented on that fact, at which – so went the rumour – the mystery man had fled into the night.

It was a good story but, like so many other good stories, belonged exclusively to the world of fiction. 'The closest inquiries have failed to confirm it,' said a railway police spokesman, with commendable restraint. Neither pub nor landlord existed except in the imagination.

Such inevitable diversions and disappointments notwithstanding, the Marshall-Robinson partnership was still in pretty good shape, and even mutually congratulatory when the inquest on Miss Camp was opened on Wednesday the 17th.

Interviewed by an impatient Press the day before, and asked whether any further clues had come to hand, the Superintendent had answered: 'Well, I can hardly give you that!'

But he had then added: 'You can say we are sifting every little fact to throw light on the matter, and that we are very pleased with the progress we have made so far. We have every reason to believe that success will be with us.'

Perhaps with a premonition of future reverses, he did not say when.

'In some respects the inquest was extremely disappointing,' one of the less responsible of the scribes who gathered at Lambeth coroner's court was later to complain. Certainly the court's extremely formal proceedings would have failed to supply his readers with anything very new.

Bar the formal identification of the victim, a description of her injuries and a visit by the jurymen to Waterloo to inspect the coach in which she had died, there was little worthwhile to report to enlighten a public eager for news of progress in the hunt for Elizabeth's killer.

And this, 'by reason of police discretion', it was said, had been conspicuously absent, although one young man who had been brought before the court was at least able to testify, all too ruefully, to the alarming side effects of police enthusiasm. '

Son of a widow – though not much help to her – who had succeeded to the management of a pub in Reading, Arthur Marshall (no relation to the Detective Inspector!) had left home unexpectedly on the morning of the day of the murder and had not returned until the night of the 15th, to find the law on his doorstep.

Seemingly an idle ne'er-do-well – 'it is nothing for him to lie in bed for weeks on end' his mother testified – young Arthur had been in minor trouble with the police at the time of his disappearance. Furthermore, on Mrs Marshall reporting his disappearance they had followed up a report that he had been seen in Guildford, where they found that, under a different name, he had been visiting a costumiers in search of a false moustache!

This, in the heat engendered by the murder search, had been sufficient for the Berkshire constabulary to put two and two together and make five, with the result that young Marshall had been given a rough ride. Only after the most merciless cross-questioning had the coroner accepted that his embarrassed explanation was genuine.

Apparently, in a belated effort to mend his ways, the lad had thought of joining the army – a whim that had since been abandoned – but had left home without telling anyone, it seemed, in order to avoid 'a row'. The moustache, he explained, had been intended to make him look less youthful and more fierce – in fact more as a soldier should.

Before the court went into a month's adjournment, there being nothing on which it could usefully proceed, the foreman of the jury voiced a question that was puzzling many a thoughtful citizen and provided at least one crust for the hungry newspapers to chew on. Why, he asked, had not the railway company offered a reward for information?

'In another notable case,' he said, with obvious reference to the apprehension of Lefroy, 'a reward led to the capture of the murderer.'

It was a valid point. The London, Brighton & South Coast Railway had offered £100 to anyone who could help trace the killer of Mr Gold. The North London Railway had done the same when confronted with Muller's murder of Mr Briggs. So why should the London & South Western hold back when it came to the need to avenge Miss Camp?

Relayed by an enthusiastic journalist to the board of the company that same day, the question received a somewhat dusty answer: 'The Directors have decided not to make the recommendation (for a reward) to such a course until they are compelled to admit themselves completely baffled.'

And, as things were, the police were 'most hopeful about the elucidation of the mystery', and the company had 'great faith in the outcome'.

To a cynical few it seemed, though probably unfairly, that such sentiments were too pious to be true: an apologia for board-room meanness. To many, it appeared that an arrest was imminent. It almost was.

The possibility that Elizabeth had been the victim of a sex-killer was still being examined by the police, but they considered it unlikely. As with the robbery theory several factors were against it.

Among the mass of the public, however, a contrary view prevailed, one more in tune with the romantic notions – and much of the popular literature – circulating in the Victorian twilight. A chaste, working-class maiden on the one side; on the other a lewd villain, a monster bent upon robbing her of her virtue or her money, and even desirous of helping himself to both. In its main ingredients the 'death before dishonour' theme evoked by Elizabeth's passing was as old as The Red Barn, but what gave it an extra piquancy was its up-to-date and familiar setting.

To many a young woman who had occasion to travel by train, the Hounslow Line murder, because of the reflections it aroused concerning the special vulnerability of her sex, was a tragedy with far more frightening and personal implications than either of its predecessors.

Yet could it be that the lessons deduced from Miss Camp's fatal journey – of the perils posed to lady travellers by wandering male villains – had been somewhat over-stressed? Was Elizabeth's encounter with her killer, whatever his motive, entirely the result of chance? Or were the blows that had battered her to death directed, not by a stranger, but by someone who knew her, someone who, perhaps, had been even close to her?

While encouraging the widest possible publicity over the search for both the murder weapon and the passengers who had travelled on the murder train, the police had also been pursuing a line of investigation on which they maintained an almost total silence. This concerned the background and habits of the deceased. It also included in its scope particulars of her family, associates and friends. Even the grief-stricken Berry had been 'checked-out' by the CID, but though ruling him out as a suspect they remained suspicious of the others who had moved in the Camp orbit.

Edward Berry, it transpired, had not been the first man in Elizabeth's life. She had previously been engaged to a barman called Brown, currently employed at the Portman Arms in the Edgware Road. Their association had been broken off after a violent argument and, so the police were told, Brown had never forgiven her.

Further inquiries on this promising theme had led to the discovery that she had recently received a number of threatening letters, and that Brown, alleged to have become insanely jealous, was believed to be their anonymous author.

Nor was this all. For someone of her age and self-acquired education, Miss Camp appeared to have been an extremely competent collector and manager of money. She never lacked it. But Brown was far less provident, almost a spendthrift, and the rumour was that he was heavily in her debt. Here, surely, was an intelligible motive.

Yet when detectives had called on him, it was to discover that this prime suspect had an unshakable alibi, one supplied by his employer, a Mr Bates. The barman had been working throughout the day of the murder, and had not once left the premises. Furthermore, for what it was worth, it appeared that Brown, and not Elizabeth, had broken off the engagement. 'Whenever we've met since then its been on cordial terms,' he said.

Coming on top of their other reverses, the officers' frustration over the collapse of the Brown hypothesis had been acute and only partly assuaged by the fact that, in the course of interrogation, the barman had been able to point to another potential suspect, this time a mysterious stranger who, so he had heard, had latterly acquired the habit of sending Elizabeth flowers, and had waited for her after closing time outside the Good Intent. But this lead, too, produced an anticlimax. The man was harmless.

However, while investigating the rumour that Brown had owed money to his former sweetheart, the CID had discovered that, whatever the truth or otherwise of his heated denials, there were others who certainly were in her debt. Among them was a brother-in-law, the husband of her younger sister; whom it will be recalled she had visited at Hammersmith before making her rendezvous at Hounslow with Mrs Haynes.

And yet another recipient of Elizabeth's bounty was a man called Thomas Stone, who on closer inspection turned out to be none other than the (euphemistically titled) 'close friend of the Haynes family', who had entertained the sisters before the train's departure. The 'celebratory drink' he had insisted on offering the 'bride-to-be' had been the last she ever tasted. Stone, it was decided, would be worth a second look.

It would appear that police patience had worn pretty thin by the time the decision was made to question Stone. Far from being solved within a matter of days, as had been confidently expected, the 'simple' Camp case looked like dragging on for ever. Every lead had terminated in a cul-de-sac.

The discovery of the bone ear-rings, on which the CID had laid such store, had been the first of many disappointments. Far from providing a clue to the identity of Miss Camp's attacker, they had turned out to have belonged to the younger sister, from whom she was said to have borrowed them shortly before her death.

Similar ill-luck had accompanied police efforts to trace the moustachioed man in the frockcoat who reportedly had left the train at Wandsworth. Unlike his Vauxhall counterpart he was known to exist, but he continued to lie low.

The pestle remained unidentified. Despite the initial jubilation that had greeted its discovery and the widespread publicity given to police appeals for information, its ownership remained an enigma. But there were still other lines of inquiry to pursue.

Berry, while expressing himself as being 'at a complete loss' as to the motive for the murder, volunteered the startling information that she 'usually carried a good deal of money'. Could it be that others – perhaps even some of the patrons of the Good Intent – had noticed this characteristic of its proprietress?

Her Hammersmith brother-in-law, manager of a prosperous store, but by no means overpaid for his services, also came under close scrutiny. He was found to be living at a level far in excess of his income, and had become heavily in debt to Elizabeth in the process.

What if the lady, on the eve of marriage, had found that she needed the money and had demanded to have it back? And what if, having known the train she would catch at Hounslow for her return home, he had joined it en route?

The personal theories of the officers in charge of the Camp investigations were not revealed at the time, and probably never will be. It is, therefore, difficult to understand just why, after extensive interviews with the extravagant brother-in-law, in which he was forced to produce his accounts and personal papers, they should have suddenly switched their inquiries to the convivial Mr Stone. But switch them they did. They took him to Hounslow police station shortly before noon 'so that he might give an explanation of his moves', and kept him there till after 5pm.

It was reported that, following his hotel session with the Haynes sisters, he had accompanied them part of the way to the station, but had then suddenly disappeared from the district, not returning till after midnight – four hours later. But of the factors that had led them to act on the assumption that, in the course of those four 'missing' hours Stone had somehow become involved in murder, the police said nothing.

A little indignantly, a *Times* correspondent pointed out that the police had effected 'what was practically the arrest of Thomas Stone', but they still kept their own counsel. Nor did the Yard attempt to quarrel with the newspaper's report that attributed to the local police the somewhat ungenerous explanation that Stone's subsequent release was because, 'there was not sufficient evidence against the man to warrant his being charged'.

The abortive interrogation of Thomas Stone was the last major move to identify Elizabeth's killer. Despite one of the most exhaustive investigations of its day, and a close working relationship between the Metropolitan and the company's police – probably unprecedented for the cordiality that existed between the partners – every effort had failed.

Like Jack the Ripper – tales of whose gruesome exploits had terrified Elizabeth – the man who had murdered Edward Berry's bride-to-be was to remain at large, free of the rope that had terminated the lives of his two predecessors, Muller and Lefroy.

Elizabeth's funeral was a grand affair. The warm-hearted Walworth Road turned out in such strength to say goodbye that 150 police, many of them mounted, were on duty to control the crowds. As the funeral procession passed towards the parish church of St Peter, hundreds of people spilled across the tram tracks to follow the cortege, bringing all other traffic to a stop. The windows and even the roofs of houses, along the route were crowded with spectators, while the church itself was filled.

The subsequent procession to Walworth Cemetery was on a similar vast scale, a *Times* reporter recording the presence of 'three mourning coaches, fifteen carriages, cabs, and other vehicles, and five omnibuses, the latter crowded with mourners'.

But as if to contrast with this extravagant parade of tribute to the bride-to-be-that-never-was, the brass plate on the coffin that reposed in the glass hearse recorded simply: 'Elizabeth Camp, aged 33 years, died February 11th 1897'.

7

The Lady Gets Her Man

For elderly Mrs Rhoda King, travelling third class on the London & South Western Railway, the journey of more than two hours from Southampton to Waterloo promised to be a bit of an ordeal.

It was Thursday 17 January 1901. The day was bitterly cold. And, as she had firmly rejected suggestions that she burden herself with a stone hot-water bottle and a travelling rug – still part of the recipe for comfort prescribed by case-hardened travellers – she would have to depend on the relatively new-fangled and notoriously inefficient steam-heating system for protection against the rigours of the weather.

Nor was she looking forward to what awaited her in London. Normally she would have been excited and happy at the prospect of visiting her son and his wife, but this was no normal reunion. They had broken the news that her grandchild had been taken seriously ill. It was therefore in a sadly reflective mood that Mrs King took her back-to-the-engine corner seat on the 11.15 (pre-noon) semi-express, and resigned herself to the tedium of the journey.

True that the lot of the traveller had improved considerably since that red-letter day when, a mere slip of a girl, she had taken her first 'ride' upon a steam train, and papa had been forced to queue at a booking-hole that bore the insulting inscription 'For Horses, Dogs, and Third-Class Passengers'. The railway company was at least more civil to its third-class passengers nowadays.

The coaches, too, were wonderfully improved. She was old enough to recall the time when the carriage floor had holes bored through it, with the purpose of 'draining the train'. Rain water, sluicing through the unglazed windows, was otherwise liable to cause a minor flood.

But, on the debit side of the new era's 'improvements', the wretched heating system of the 11.15 had broken down – just as her husband had anticipated it would – and she couldn't see out through the glass it was so thickly coated with frost. Worse, she had just heard at the barrier that the journey would take even longer than was scheduled. The inclement weather would delay the train at every stop.

It was at the first of these, at Eastleigh, junction for the line to Gosport via Fareham, that the tactful stranger entered the compartment, which, until that moment, Mrs King had occupied by herself. A tall, handsome young man in his early twenties, and, from his appearance, apparently well-to-do, the new arrival chose, as she had done, a corner seat, and, after a moment's hesitation, seated himself also with his back to the engine, a move for which the lady was duly grateful. It was embarrassing, when travelling unescorted, to have to meet the gaze of a strange gentleman face to face, and it was thoughtful of him to have appreciated that fact.

Mrs King was not to know that the newcomer, George Parker, carried a loaded revolver in his pocket, or that she was to be one of his two human targets.

Whatever the public's reservations about the benefits of the new carriage heating systems, there was no doubt that the 1890s had seen some extraordinary improvements in passenger comfort, and none of them more pronounced than in respect of what, for want of a better phrase, could be called the 'domestic arrangements'.

Until the start of the decade, a major dread of the shy traveller was of being 'taken short' in the course of the journey, the railway companies providing no facilities to cope with that contingency. And while a gentleman might succeed in avoiding too shocking a breach of public decorum by utilising, though only after the most skilled and complicated of manoeuvres, one of the thick paper bags that were offered for the purpose, for the ladies – quite obviously – there could be no such easy relief.

In recent years, however, effective steps had been taken to solve their embarrassing problem. Some companies had introduced the corridor coach, equipped with a lavatory at the end of the corridor, while others had provided the older-style individual compartments with 'lavatory chambers' (partitioned cubicles) of their own. It was in such a prudently equipped compartment – its facilities only a door's thickness away – that Mrs King had installed herself.

Photographs taken in the 1880s of a third class railway compartment and, overleaf, a first class compartment.

Farmer Pearson joined the train at its next stop, Winchester. A burly old gentleman, whose ruddy cheeks and heavy gait almost caricatured his calling, he sat himself down in the carriage's right-hand corner, and after a cursory, but genial nod to his fellow occupants, stuck his nose close to the text of his open newspaper.

A little later, after a leisurely perusal of the 'mopping-up' operations being undertaken against the Boers in South Africa and a critical look at the 'hunting appointments' column, he methodically folded the paper, put it down on the seat beside him, closed his eyes and nodded peacefully off to sleep. He was to stay that way until he died.

The sky had begun to brighten as the train left Hampshire behind, and now, just short of Surbiton, the windows were almost frost-free. Mrs King had turned her back on the carriage and her two companions, and was looking out at the Surrey countryside when she became casually aware that the young man had got to his feet and gone into the lavatory chamber. She was still looking out at the countryside when he emerged a few minutes later, and therefore never noticed he had a revolver in his hand.

Passengers enjoying the comforts of a first class railway compartment at night.

Two sharp reports. A numbing blow to the side of her face! Dazed, she swung round, clapped her hand to the source of the pain, and found that her fingers were sticky with blood. It came from a deep gash in her cheek and red spots were falling on the collar of her new black coat. She saw the tactful stranger bending over the old farmer who, she realised, was very probably dead.

'My God! What have you done?' she screamed. With one hand already groping in Pearson's pocket, the young man employed the other to point the revolver at her.

As if in a trance he answered, without expression, 'I did it for money. I have need of money.' He added as if a casual afterthought, 'Have you got any?'

It was as Mrs King was fumbling shakily in her purse that she noticed the blood running down the farmer's face. He had been shot in the eye and death must have been instantaneous, yet a gurgling noise was emerging from his throat. It was horrifying. Quite uncanny. Momentarily she felt that she was about to swoon, but realised that swooning would not do.

Instead, forcing herself to look directly at the killer and throttling down the hysteria that threatened to overwhelm her, she said levelly, 'Do you not think it would be better to cover his face?

There was the briefest of silences, broken only by the careless rhythm of the train and the screech of the engine whistle, as it prepared to round the bend.

'Perhaps he will lose his balance,' Mrs King thought wildly. 'Perhaps he will slip and fall.' But of course he did not. Parker, as she was later to know him, was continuing to rummage through the dead man's pockets. 'Don't you think,' she repeated slowly, 'it would be better to cover his face?' Another pause until, to her astonished relief, he lowered the revolver and produced a pocket handkerchief. This he threw across the gaping wound on his victim's face as casually as another might apply a sheet of blotting paper to a patch of spilled ink. 'You must keep quiet or I'll kill you, too,' he said.

Mrs King felt her terror subside, though only slightly. A moment before she had thought that he was bound to kill her anyway. 'Of course I'll keep quiet', she answered.

More silence, followed by a mumble of self-congratulation as Parker at last came to grips with what he wanted – Pearson's purse. Laying the revolver on the seat, he opened the purse, glanced at its contents, extracted a golden sovereign and unexpectedly proffered it to the astonished Mrs King. 'Would this be of any use to you?' he asked. 'You'd better take it.'

It was almost the last straw and she yelled at him. 'Of course I won't. I don't want it!'

But then, as he grabbed the gun and she saw its muzzle swing toward her once again, her anger and courage were submerged by fear. 'Don't shoot!' she cried. 'For God's sake don't shoot me.'

In desperation, she threw out her arms in an imploring gesture, her hands still bloody from the wound in her cheek, and he jerked away from her as if in sudden revulsion. 'Don't touch me,' he snapped, and then, in a gentler tone, 'I'm sorry if I hurt you. Just keep very quiet and I won't hurt you again.'

She kept very quiet.

The revolver that was to bring death to Farmer Pearson had been purchased by his killer in Bernard Street, Southampton, for the not exorbitant sum of 7s 5d, ammunition included. At the time he intended – or so he said later – to use it on the girl-friend he had left waiting in the private bar of the cheap hotel where they had spent the night together, and then turn it against himself. It had seemed the best he could do for both of them. He was unemployed and 'desperate'. She had an unhappy marriage to a soldier stationed in India. And, if he did not get a favourable reply from his father to whom he had written asking for money, they might as well end it all.

But whatever the truth of this account of the purpose of his purchase, one thing appears certain: Parker's career, as he had often said, had been 'no bloody bed of roses'.

One of a family of eight children, this son of a Warwickshire labourer had come up the hard way and had continued to do things the hard way ever since. Sent to a reformatory when only fourteen, and reputedly made the tougher by this experience, he had not been content on his release to keep his nose clean and stay quietly at home, in fact, 'home' – except in name – no longer existed.

Plagued by the pains of poverty, and its palliative, drink, his parents had long since ceased to be civil to each other and the family was breaking up. For nearly a month George endured their mutual feuding, and then, having quarrelled with both, had disappeared into the blue, enlisting in the Royal Marine Artillery. The Royal Marines, it was said, could make or break a man. And Marine Parker, enlisted under the name of Hill, certainly underwent a change while in the corps.

It smartened him up, both physically and mentally. It turned a loutish village lay-about into an arresting figure of a man, straight-backed and alert. But it also served to bring to the surface what was to prove his fundamental weakness – vanity. He had an obsessive desire to cut a dash amongst his fellows, and a propensity for womanising among the more precocious, and expensive, of the sex. With only the serviceman's shilling a day to subsidise such ambitious tastes, George Henry Parker, alias Hill, had set himself firmly on the road to disaster.

It was at Portsmouth Barracks that the service career of this handsome, swashbuckling six-footer came to an abrupt and pitiable end when he stood accused of the unforgivable offence: 'stealing from a comrade'.

It had been alleged, despite his denials, that he had stolen letters addressed to fellow members in the corps, opened them up and extracted money and postal orders. He was also alleged to have forged their signatures in order to cash the orders, though on this latter score a magistrates' court declined to convict.

Comparing his punishment – three weeks imprisonment on the theft charge – with that imposed on others by the tough justice of the time, Parker had cause to consider himself extremely lucky, but he did not. For the effect of the conviction, allied to the nature of the crime, meant also his discharge from the Royal Marines, 'Services no longer required'.

The route that was to lead George Henry Parker from the barrack-room at Portsmouth to Eastleigh railway station, and the compartment wherein sat the unsuspecting Mrs King, was to prove remarkably circuitous. Though many of the details of his journey remain unknown, it would appear to have taken him first to London, and thence, to judge by appearances, to a reasonably profitable association with the London underworld in various capacities.

Indeed, there were times when visiting his old haunts in Southampton and Portsmouth that this expensively dressed and newly well-breeched young man appeared to be more cut out for the role of conquering hero than that of a broken marine. He was once heard to boast that he was 'rolling in money, and very keen to spend it'. Needless to say, there were plenty who helped him to do so. On another occasion his triumphal progress was interrupted only by the need to evade the attentions of the Portsmouth police, acting on a request from the Metropolitan Police to detain him for questioning over a robbery at the Lyceum Theatre, London. And when, on Saturday 12 January he called on his sweetheart, Lizzie Rowland, at her Eastney home, George Parker looked the very picture of prosperity.

It was an unlikely sort of romance, this association between the handsome, highly experienced philanderer, and the simple, rather plain-looking laundry girl, wife of a private of the Scottish Rifles then stationed in India. Yet it was probably the nearest thing to love that George Parker would ever know, while for Lizzie the next four days were uninterrupted bliss.

It was for her, unhappily married and with no close friends or relations, that George, unemployed and without prospects despite his brave appearance, had rashly returned to Portsmouth, though still 'wanted' in connection with the Lyceum affair. It was also for her that, in their four days together, he spent every penny of what little remained of the opulence that had so dazzled his more casual acquaintances only a few months earlier. And it was for her that he was to write, while awaiting trial for his life, 'It makes my heart bleed for you ... to think that I shall never see you again, and that you will be alone and miserable'.

But this sentimental composition – in effect his valediction – was still a week away when, on the morning of the 17th, his newly purchased revolver in his pocket and suffering from a hangover from the night before, he broke the news to the bewildered girl that despite his wealthy appearance, he was broke, flat broke. He had only sufficient money left to pay her fare back to Portsmouth.

When they parted at Eastleigh Junction, George Parker was near to murder.

'Keep very quiet ...' the man had warned her.

There were times when Mrs King was almost persuaded that she was living in a dream – or rather, nightmare. That what was happening to her could not possibly be real. A corpse, still bleeding, in one corner of a railway carriage. An armed gunman, his murderer, in another. And herself sitting taut and upright, with her back to the wall, trying to keep her knees from knocking, wondering when she would die. Surely the nightmare could not last? Surely someone would shake her awake?

Noisily, importantly, with seeming indifference to her plight, the train was passing through the outer suburbs, but for all the good that it was likely to do her, it might just as well have been journeying to the moon. She saw shops and houses, and little back gardens, and leafless apple trees, the frost on branches still unthawed ... and she wondered if she would ever see them again.

There was a glimpse of children in scarves and mufflers, grouped on a bridge above the track and waving to the train so frantically you would have thought they had never seen its like before ... the dull blur of a woman's head framed in a scullery window, and bowed over the crockery piled high in the sink ... and at one point a policeman stood, plump, solemn, and benign ... but these were all outside, a world away.

'Keep very quiet ...' She had obeyed the order. She was still obeying it. It was Parker who was the talkative one, rambling on and on and on. Telling her that he had been a soldier, and wanted to go to South Africa. Telling her that he had had 'nothing but bad luck'.

'Keep very quiet?' The thought crossed her mind that he almost seemed to need her. That he desperately needed someone, someone with whom to talk, someone to justify himself to. His mother maybe? But then, with that pitying thought her gaze fell upon the farmer, his body tilting from one side to another with the rocking of the train, and all her fears returned to her.

Remorse for having killed Pearson, self-pity at being the underdog, almost maniacal exaltation – the man's mood swung like a weathercock.

'I've a damned good mind to put it in his hand.' It was Parker again fingering his jaw and looking worriedly at his victim.

'What do you mean?' she asked.

'The revolver. If I put it in his hands they will think he did it himself.'

It was preposterous. Absurd. So infantile that she wondered how he could have thought of it. A suicide? Did he seriously think that 'they' wouldn't notice her own wound?

But already Parker's restless mood had changed again, and this time to near-despair. 'Promise you wont say anything?' he said.

'I promise,' she answered.

Abandoning his great project of transforming Pearson's murder into 'suicide', Parker glanced helplessly at the corpse, helplessly at the gun, and then helplessly back to Mrs King. 'I don't know what to do with this damned revolver. I mustn't keep it about me.'

'Then why not get rid of it', she suggested.

Had anyone suggested to the neighbours, back home in Exmoor Road, that Mrs Rhoda King was a woman of extraordinary courage and resource, their reaction would have been one of polite disbelief. A good mother, yes; she had a lovely family. And for a grandmother, she had kept her looks. A pleasant soul, undoubtedly. Few people could dislike her. But really there was little that was remarkable about her. And Mrs King would have echoed this opinion; no heroine she. Even now, as she conceived her preposterous plan, it was cowardice rather than courage, so she felt, that lent her strength and cunning.

'If I were you,' she said, 'I would throw the revolver out of the window.'

It was indeed a most preposterous plan, and its motives surely must be so transparently plain that, for all she knew, his answer would be a bullet in her head. But, having opened the dialogue, she had no recourse but to sustain it, and make the grotesque and implausible appear reasonable and convincing.

'Once you've disposed of it,' she elaborated, 'no one is going to know.'

For a moment, as his moody gaze surveyed her, she felt the man had rumbled her deceit, and braced herself instinctively against violence to come. But then, as if to himself, he mumbled, 'After all, wouldn't do for the police to find it.'

He continued to regard her moodily, still irresolute before, as if on impulse he dropped the window down. But then, with equal suddenness, he slammed it shut again. As he turned towards her she saw to her dismay that he was still holding the gun.

'I can't do it here,' he explained. 'There are men working on the track. They're sure to spot me if I throw it out now.'

'Well, why not try again a little further on?' So effectively did she mask her agitation that the suggestion sounded almost casual, and from Parker came a meek nod of assent.

Just what had happened to the cool and collected killer of some minutes back? Hesitant, fumbling, an almost futile figure – this wasn't the man at all. But how long would it last, his apparent vulnerability? And what could she expect when the train reached Vauxhall? If this creature of moods should have the gun still in his hands when, as planned, he made his bid for freedom, might he not use it to silence the one witness to his crime? Once more Mrs King had to cope with, and overcome, the fear that brought the sickness into her throat, before reassuming her role of guide, philosopher and friend.

The 11.15 (semi-express) from Southampton to London was almost within sight of its destination when Parker, pulled down the window and hurled the revolver to the far side of the track.

The passenger was in such a hurry to leave the up-train from Southampton on its arrival at Vauxhall that he threw open the door of the compartment and stepped on to the footboard when it was still far short of the station. He jumped on to the platform before the train had come to a stop. Now, as he dashed for the stairs that led down to the exit, he almost collided with a porter, Bill Craig, but spared no apology: evidently time was too precious.

Nor did Craig's expostulations at this heedless conduct go to more than a sharp epithet or two, his attention having been diverted to the lady who had appeared in the doorway of the compartment that the man had just vacated. She was waving her arms and shouting, appeared to be in an awful state, but her words were not readily comprehensible and it took him a few seconds to realise their import.

'Murder!' she was shouting. 'Stop that man!' And then, seeing him hesitate, she added: 'Stop that man! He has murdered someone!'

Abandoning his trolley, Craig gave chase, two or three other workers following at his heels.

Whatever else the Royal Marines may have neglected in the education of George Parker, they had certainly ensured that he was physically fit. He had gone down the stairs at speed, brushed aside the collector at the barrier at the bottom, and was now bolting along the street outside. As Craig, more easily winded, paused briefly to shout for assistance from passers-by, he was suddenly aware that he was no longer in the lead of the pursuit.

A police officer – PC Thomas Fuller – had appeared at the far end of the street, right in the path of the fugitive who, his escape route barred in that direction, turned left and in desperation ran through the entrance to the gas works. The PC, the railway workers, a couple of carters abandoning their carts and a coster leaving his barrow – it was an enthusiastic pack that followed Parker's trail. But despite their numbers, augmented by employees of the plant itself, the chase was hard.

Sprawling along the Thames-side, interlaced by railway tracks, coal dumps, sheds and retort houses the gas works was a regular warren, and their man adroit in employing its complexities to advantage. At one stage Craig caught a glimpse of him scurrying into a retort house but, when he followed, lost him in the inky blackness. Later he was seen doubling back to the gas works gate, perhaps with the intention of scaling the wall nearby and, though headed off, again succeeded in vanishing. But, protract it though he might, this game of hide-and-seek could have only one ending, and the end for Parker came when a fire-raker at the works spotted him lurking behind a truck.

No resistance was offered to PC Fuller as he made his arrest, the most noteworthy in his career. Parker seemed to accept it as inevitable, and said nothing as the handcuffs were clamped around his wrists. But despite his soldier-like assumption of indifference to his captors it was soon evident that his thoughts were black and bitter. First words when he eventually broke silence were: 'I wish I had killed that woman …'. Everyone knew who he meant.

Whatever he may have felt about Mrs King during the train journey, there was no doubt about George Parker's indignation at the part she had played in bringing him to justice. Neither was there any doubt that he regretted 'his mistake' in sparing her from the fate of the murdered Pearson. 'Had I killed her, too, I would have got away', he told PC Fuller when he was led away to Larkshall Lane police station.

In fact, so disgusted was he at the way in which his 'soft-heartedness', as he saw it, had served to overcome his better judgement that he tended to overlook the fact that it was the lady, not he, who was the 'injured' party.

The courage that had sustained Mrs King throughout the most critical moments of her ordeal – moments when her life hung in the balance – had deserted her at the moment of relief. No sooner had she realised that her captor was in flight, and that her cries had been heard and had set others in pursuit of him, than the full awareness of the extent of the dangers she had endured swept over her, setting her knees shaking and turning her stomach.

As she tried to tell the sympathetic crowd, now mulling around her on the platform, the story of what had happened, the words came out in a meaningless babble, and suddenly it was all too much for her to bear.

Someone yelled, 'Give her air l' Someone else went for their smelling salts, and a male traveller pulled out a brandy flask. But all of them were too late. Mrs King had collapsed.

Rushed to St Thomas' Hospital she was found to be suffering from the effects of her wounds and delayed shock. The bullet had entered her cheek at a point just behind the jawbone. Fired at close range, it had broken in three, and had left a powder mark as a blemish that was to stay with her all her life. The bone itself had not been damaged and the doctors were able to declare that there would be no permanent physical injury.

Mentally, however, the shock had been extreme. She could not bear to talk of her experience, all she could say was that a man had shot at her. Attempts to get her to elaborate on the details were met by a flood of tears and the reference to Pearson's death so upset her that it was decided to postpone any further questioning until she had fully recovered. For whatever else was uncertain, one thing was all too clear: Mrs King was in no state to appear in court, and would not be so for some time to come.

Meanwhile, unknown to her, false rumours of the tragedy that were circulating in Southampton had resulted in its claiming another casualty – her husband. Informed that his wife was dead he, too, had collapsed, and had to receive medical attention.

Parker appeared at Westminster Police Court the following day, charged with 'the murder on the London and South Western Railway of Mr William Pearson, by shooting him in a carriage between Surbiton and Vauxhall'. The case was adjourned for a week and the prisoner remanded in custody.

During his interrogation he had astonished detectives by the light-hearted way he appeared to regard the charge against him, reportedly 'laughing and joking' as they questioned him, and in court he displayed a similar bravado.

On his next appearance, however, on Friday the 25th, a *Times* reporter remarked; 'The defiant swaggering manner which first characterised him had disappeared. He now looked down in the dock and appeared to feel his position.'

Also indicative of a change of heart – or change of front – on the part of the erstwhile 'hard case' was a letter he wrote to his father in which he confessed his guilt, asked for forgiveness, and urged that his fate be held up as an awful warning to the rest of the family on the evils of craving for money.

'Let all my brothers and sisters read this, and tell them to take advice from me,' he wrote. 'Live a straight-forward and happy life. Never crave for money. It is that which has been the ruination of my life.'

Worthy sentiments they may be, but especially gratifying to Victorian moralists who always liked to see a sinner repent before they hanged him. There were some, however, who read a little more into the Parker letter, and suspected that, in part at least, it was not so much a product of genuine contrition as an attempt to transfer the blame.

'I must have been mad,' he stated. 'I do not know what I did it for. I had no cause. I believe I am going mad.'

All the same, although assuring his parent that 'I do not want to hurt your feelings in any way', he was not above dropping a hint of

The Black Maria, 1887.

yet another circumstance that might serve to help extenuate his crime: 'Had you not broken up the home while I was in the Royal Marine Light Infantry, I might have been a better man.'

'Pretty girls', it appeared, had also contributed to leading George astray. 'Do not be led away by girls' looks', was his advice to the family. 'Pretty girls I mean. It is through them that I have been in so much trouble. I have been so easily led by them.'

Indeed, the only person to emerge with any credit from his apologia was the unlikely Lizzie, 'whom I love better than gold, and she is not good looking; but I love her dearly and she does me'. He was, he said, afraid that she would now 'destroy herself'.

This note to Parker senior from 'your wretched and heartbroken son' was one of three widely publicised letters composed by the prisoner while awaiting trial.'

'Dearest Lizzie,' he wrote to the lonely Lizzie Rowland, 'It makes my heart bleed for you, as I am writing these few lines, to think that I shall never see you again, and that you will be alone and miserable now, and through me. I always loved you dearly ...'

The picture he conveyed of himself was a moving one, thoroughly miserable because of the 'false charges' that had caused him to be drummed out of the Marines – 'God knows I was as innocent as the dead'.

He had purchased the revolver 'so that when I came down to Portsmouth on the Saturday I could end both our lives if I had not been successful in obtaining money from my father.'

But probably the most remarkable of the 'repentant' gunman's epistles was that addressed to the wife of the man he had murdered. To her he wrote: 'I am writing these few lines to you to ask your forgiveness for the crime which I have done. I read an account of your husband's funeral in the paper. I am really truly sorry, and I feel for you and your husband's brother. I am truly sorry and repentant for having, in an evil moment, allowed myself to be carried away into committing the offence with which I now stand charged.'

He had no intention whatever of shooting her husband, he assured the widow, but had purchased the revolver with the intention of 'shooting the girl I had been going out with, and myself. She was unhappy at home, and so was I. I shot your husband on the spur of the moment.'

Signing himself the 'wretched murderer of your husband', he entreated her to 'write me a few lines and say that you forgive me'. 'I must have been mad. I do not know what I did it for. I had no cause. I believe I'm going mad.' More – far more – was to be heard of the 'madness' referred to in Parker's letter to his father, and the 'spur of the moment' excuse advanced to Pearson's widow. It formed the basis of his defence when, at the Central Criminal Court, he unexpectedly altered his plea to 'not guilty'.

It was argued that, although he had confessed to the murder, his chronic alcoholism had prevented his being in his right mind at the time he committed it. Unfortunately for the prisoner, however, Mrs King, restored to health, was to testify that his behaviour, however variable, was far removed from that of a mindless drunk.

But even more unfortunate for the defence was the fact that, just prior to making his escape bid at Vauxhall, the 'mad' George Parker had remembered that his railway ticket only covered the journey from Southampton to Eastleigh, and had coolly helped himself to the dead man's ticket instead. This calm and calculating action, argued the prosecution, was scarcely the act of a man who reputedly was 'out of his mind' at the time, but that of a cold-blooded killer. It was a premise with which both judge and jury agreed.

Parker was hanged three weeks later.

8

Terminus

To a minority of early Victorians the railway train was an abomination. 'We should as soon expect the people of Woolwich to suffer themselves to be fired-off upon one of Congreve's ricochet rockets as trust themselves to the mercy of such a machine going at such a rate,' wrote a contributor to the *Saturday Review*, appalled by 'the palpably ridiculous prospect held out of locomotives travelling twice as fast as stage coaches'.

Most preferred to share the view expressed by contemporary historian and loco-lover Scott Walker: that they were witnessing: 'The greatest national triumph of the age, which for speed, elegance and economy is altogether novel and astonishing.'

True, Mr Walker's attendant eulogy of the railway engine – 'a charger snorting steam and fire' – seemed to some to be a little high-flown, while his praise for the railway carriages of his time as 'proceeding with a sudden and agreeable velocity, becoming, as it were, the tail of a comet' would certainly qualify, if repeated today, as an offence against the Trades Descriptions Act. But such reservations apart, rail travel was fast becoming a part of the British way of life, with even the young Victoria, after her first ride on the Iron Way in 1842, confiding to King Leopold: 'I am quite charmed by it.'

It was left to Thackeray, twenty years later, to give voice to the possibility that the enclosed and corridorless compartments that made up Scott Walker's 'comet' could be death traps for the lone passenger, offering an ideal setting for murder.

'Have you', he wrote in the December 1862 issue of Cornhill, 'ever entered a first-class railway carriage where an old gentleman sat alone in a sweet sleep, daintily murdered him, taken his pocketbook and got out at the next station? You know that this circumstance occured in France a few months since?'

Inspiring the sage's comment was the murder of M. Poinsot, a French magistrate shot and clubbed to death on the Troyes-Paris night express. Thackeray's implication was that the British traveller by train could not forever hope to remain immune from a form of crime that had become quite commonplace on the Continent.

Even though the Poinsot affair created a stir at the time, not only because of the victim's rank – he was president of one of the chambers of the Imperial Court – but also because of dark whispers from the Sûreté that his killer could have been a Prussian spy, Thackeray's warning passed unheeded until, less than two years later, that very British 'old gentleman' Thomas Briggs, on that almost eccentrically British North London Railway shared the magistrate's tragic fate.

The Briggs murder, Gold's murder, the murders of Miss Camp and Farmer Pearson – each aroused public panic, but a panic that quickly subsided, and was tempered by the thought that such incidents were rare indeed compared with the toll exacted across the Channel. By the turn of the century there had been four train murders in England. In France alone the tally was twenty-four.

When George Parker's trial was nearing its conclusion newspaper reports of the court's proceedings wore a border of black. But this, however appropriate, had nothing at all to do with the killer's ultimate fate. Instead, it was to mourn the death of Queen Victoria, an enthusiast for rail travel from the days when it was still a novelty for the few, to its heyday as a force that had reshaped the geography of Britain and linked the outposts of an Empire that covered a quarter of the globe.

Parker's crime had been the last of its kind to be committed during the Queen's long reign. And, like its predecessors, it was followed by an intensification of the railway companies' efforts to keep their clients safe from future outrage and the fate – that terrible fate – 'of a victim at once caged and hunted'.

Although the oil-lamps and gas mantles, Muller 'lights' and hopeful 'rope alarms' have since passed away with the 'iron charger' itself, the Victorian train murderer lives on in the deeds of his successors. In 1976 alone, British Rail and London Transport trains witnessed as many murders – four – as their primitive forebears had seen perpetrated over three-quarters of a century. And also registered to the railways' debit were eight attempted murders, six manslaughters, 38 instances of grievous bodily harm, 86 cases of malicious wounding, 16 rapes and 175 indecent assaults.

A far way to travel, one might feel, from that day in a crowded Old Bailey court, with a young man called Muller on trial for his life, when a solicitor general pronounced to an awed and receptive jury: 'If there is any occasion when a man may consider himself perfectly safe, it is when he is travelling in a first-class railway carriage ...'

Bibliography

The Annual Registry (1860)
The Annual Registry (1864)
Aldick, Richard D. *Victorian Studies in Scarlet* (J. M. Dent, 1972)
Course, E. A. *London Railways* (Batsford, 1962)
Course, Edwin *The Railways of Southern England* (Batsford, 1973)
Ferneyhough, Frank *Steam Trains Down the Line* (Tyndall, 1975)
Hamiltop Ellis, C. *Steam Railways* (Eyre Methuen, 1975)
Irving, H. B. *The Trial of Franz Muller* (Wm Hodge & Company, 1911)
Jackson, Alan A. *London's Local Railways* (David & Charles, 1978)
Lustgarten, Edgar *A Century of Murderers* (Eyre Methuen, 1975)
Pile's Directory (1881)
Robbins, Michael *The North London Railway* (Oakwood Press, 1967)
Rolt, L. T. C., with revised material by G. M. Kichenside, *Red for Danger* (David & Charles, 1976)
Smullen, Ivor *Taken for a Ride* (Jenkins, 1968)
—*Things Not Generally Known* (second edition 1861)
Whitbread, J. R. *The Railway Policeman* (Harrap, 1961)
White, H. P. A *Regional History of the Railways of Great Britain* Vol II *Southern England* (David & Charles, 1964)
  Vol III *Greater London* (David & Charles, 1971)
Williams, R. A. *The London & South Western Railway* Vols I & II (David & Charles, 1968, 1973)

Index

Futher titles from Amberley Publishing:

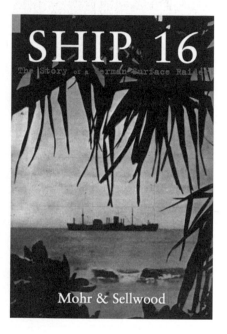

978-1-84868-1156
The story of Nazi Germany's most successful commerce raider of World War Two, sinking over 160,000 tons of Allied shipping. Told by First Officer Heinrich Mohr.

978-1-84868-2450
A vivid account of the world's strangest pit disaster. Written by a husband and wife team who interviewed the survivors and rescue workers involved in this terrible disaster.

978-1-84868-0937
The first fully-illustrated version of Col. Archibald Gracie's probing and insightful survivor memoir.

978-1-84868-0531
Myers' sensational account, published barely weeks after the ship sank and a classic of disaster literature.

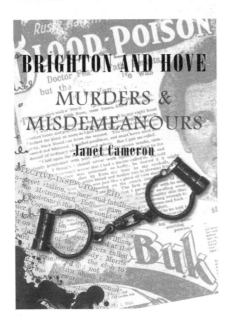

Amberley's *Murders & Misdemeanours* series explores the UK's dark history of crime and punishment.

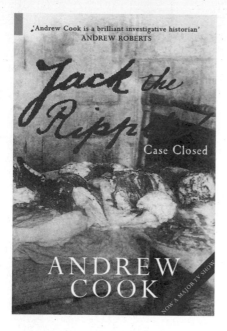

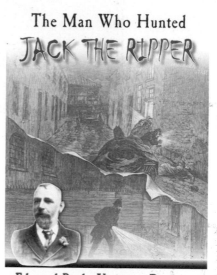

978-1-84868-3273
Finally solves the mystery of the Victorian serial killer who murdered and mutilated up to eleven women in 1888.

978-1-84868-2603
A fascinating account of victorian murder investigation, by two of Britain's most respected Ripperologists.

The ghostly counterpart to *Murders & Misdemeanors*, Amberley's *Paranormal* series explores the chilling paranormal phenomena witnessed thoughout the UK.